THE REVOLUTION
OF THE
LATIN AMERICAN CHURCH

THE REVOLUTION
OF THE
LATIN AMERICAN
CHURCH

by Hugo Latorre Cabal

Translated from the Spanish by
Frances K. Hendricks and Beatrice Berler

University of Oklahoma Press: Norman

Books by Hugo Latorre Cabal
La Hispanidad (Bogotá, 1950)
Mi Novela (Bogotá, 1961)
El Comandante Guevera en Punta del Este (Bogotá, 1961)
The Revolution of the Latin American Church (Norman, 1978)

Library of Congress Cataloging in Publication Data

Latorre Cabal, Hugo.
    The revolution of the Latin American church.

    Translation of La revolución de la iglesia latino-americana.
    1. Catholic Church in Latin America—History.
I. Title.
BX1426.2.L33513   282'.8   77-9117
ISBN 0-8061-1449-5

Copyright 1978 by the University of Oklahoma Press,
Publishing Division of the University.
Manufactured in the U.S.A.

Table of Contents

"Any cultivated man is a theologian,
and to be one, faith is not indispensable."

Jorge Luis Borges

THE REVOLUTION
OF THE
LATIN AMERICAN CHURCH

From Pope Alexander VI to Pope John XXIII

Conformists and rebels disembarked together on that day of discovery. After land had been sighted from the *Pinta,* the chief of the expedition in his admiral's array, with Christ's standard in one hand and the insignia of the Catholic monarchs in the other, took possession of the new territory with Portuguese pomp in the name of the Church and State made one by theology and law. He proclaimed, "Our Redeemer gave this victory to our own most illustrious King and Queen and to their Kingdoms famous for such a noble cause, therefore all Christianity should rejoice and celebrate great festivals and give solemn thanks for an achievement which will join so many people to our Holy Faith."

The Indies—Latin America—became the bastion of dogmatism for the Bishop of Rome and a suffering part of the Spanish existence. In the same year Ferdinand and Isabella had given thanks to God for victory over Mohammed and for the gift of the New World. Called upon to ratify these divine intentions, without, however, being clearly independent of the temporal powers (Spain, Portugal, and France), the venerated, yet manipulated and chastised Vicar of Christ on Earth legitimated the rights of the Spanish crown to the Indies. Since Columbus' action at Guanahaní was provisional only, it was necessary to obtain juridical confirmation with ecumenical validity for the claim to all he had discovered.

As only the Pope could provide such a title, the two naval powers, both Catholic and imperial, applied to Alexander VI, the most controversial of all popes, to determine the respective rights in the New World of his most powerful vassals and greatest sources of income. Though Ferdinand and Isabella had Columbus' discovery in their favor, John II of Portugal had an authorization from the previous Pope to discover lands within an immense and poorly defined area which, apparently, the Spanish were wrongfully invading.

Spain, just as Catholic as Portugal but more powerful, had the advantage in that arbitration. Alexander VI was a Borgia from Valencia. On May 4, 1493 he issued the bull *Inter Coetera* dividing the non-Christian world between the two powers along an imaginary line one hundred leagues west of the Cape Verde Islands. The bull did not satisfy John II, but it was morally and juridically adequate to sanctify the Spanish title to the Indies. The Holy See made the Spanish crown the owner of Latin America with full jurisdiction and absolute authority. By fulfilling its obligation of converting the aboriginal peoples to the Catholic faith, the crown was able to establish its exploitation of the New World. Church and State, perniciously overlapping, tended in the ensuing centuries to fuse the interests of the bishops and the *encomenderos* (holders of right to tribute from the Indians).

A year after Christopher Columbus' disembarcation at Guanahaní, the papacy, exercising its function as the highest international tribunal, extended its exclusive prerogatives over the consciences, lives, and well-being of the men of the New World Spain had discovered. The immediate exercise of the right opened discussions between two well-defined wings of the Church.

On returning from his first voyage Columbus paraded several aborigines, part of Spain's booty, through the streets of Seville and Barcelona. Differences of opinion, which would become a resounding public controversy, immediately broke out. Those said to be, sincerely or falsely, defenders of religion upheld the opinions of Pedro Mártir of Anglería that "never had God created men more steeped in vices and bestialities, without any leavening of goodness or good breeding," and of Sepúlveda that "the coarseness of their wits, their servile and barbarous nature make them subject to those more advanced, like the Spanish." In connection with the concept of the "noble savage," rationalists developed a whole ideology supported in their *Annual Relations* by the Jesuits who exalted the good features of the aborigines and even justified their negative aspects.

After his second voyage Columbus dispatched a cargo of indigenous people to the Peninsula to be sold. The crown sanctioned the proposal on April 12, 1495. The next day, however, another royal disposition ordered that the money received from the sale be retained until theologians had clarified the issue of the morality of the transaction—the first manifestation of a controversy which was to intensify with the passage of time; this was the first episode in the long struggle for justice in Latin America, the baptismal ceremony of the Old Church and the New Church.

The unity of Castile in the name of the Catholic faith followed the victory over the Arabs, the persecution of the Jews, and the recovery of the fiefs, all in the name of protection of the Catholic faith. Men prided themselves on their purity of doctrine, became fanatics, and grew rich. The Spanish had also become a "nation of theologians"—the wise men of the 1500's—and a nation of mystics—saints of the *Siglo de Oro.*

At the time of the conquest, ecclesiastics in Spain and America reflected different faces of Spain. Some theologians and holy men sided with the oppressed, representing from that time the rebel Church, while the great churchmen and many chaplains of the expeditions of conquest were with the oppressors and represented the conformist Church.

Exemplifying the rebel Church, a Dominican friar, Francisco de Vitoria, impugned the Spanish emperor's claim to the right to take land from the people and press them into bondage. He condemned the unjust war; he absolved the aborigines from the sin of irreligion; and he denied that the pope had civil and political sovereignty in the temporal realm. Another, Fray Antonio de Montesinos, directed his indignation at the Church for failing to suppress the cruelty of the first settlers from Spain. From the pulpit he denounced their merciless treatment of the Indians, stating that because of such treatment they had forfeited their hope of eternal salvation.

In the same revolutionary spirit, the Jesuit Juan de Mariana justified tyrannicide. Juan Luis Vives, a pacifist and a witness of the misery of his times, and to a small degree initiator of modern psychology, said with respect to the Inquisition, "we have, in truth, the souls of torturers." There was also Francisco Suárez who laid down the proper limits of Church and State, and based liberty on the social contract. Others, too, worked the furrow opened by Erasmus for "new Christians."

The Spanish humanist current persisted throughout the period of conquest and colonization, and during the republican epoch as well, expressed by clergy who denounced the infamy hidden by a semblance of grandeur. Some clergy actively and directly attacked slavery and the misery inflicted on the aborigines. When Charles III expelled the Jesuits in 1767, he turned them into active agents of sedition. Father Pablo Vizcardo Guzmán, creole of Arequipa, Perú, launched a revolutionary program, entrusting its spread to English Protestants, allies of American liberty, the resentful lower clergy, and the proscribed Jesuits. Within the humanist element of the Latin American Church, the minority turned to medieval piety through the Franciscanism which licked the sores of the slaves and led them to the altars.

But Antonio de Montesinos, Bartolomé de las Casas, Antonio de Vieyra, and Luis Beltrán, among others, denounced and opposed the oppressive system, demanding change. They launched their attack against the arrogant authority of the nobles and the Indian *caciques* who joined forces with the high ecclesiastical dignitaries. Toribio de Benavente, the Jesuit Manoel Nóbrega, Pedro de Gante, Alonso Sandoval, and Pedro Claver found balms for misery and escape from reality in their visionary spirituality. They sought to smooth rocky ways with compassion and piety. Though they endeavored to assuage the pain of wounds with the daily miracle of love, they looked upon the causes of those wounds with resignation.

That was not the case with the others, the fighting rebels. Witness a sermon preached to the island's settlers by Antonio de Montesinos in a rude church in Española. Just a few years after the discovery, the Dominican thundered,

Tell me by what right and under what law do you hold these Indians in such cruel and horrible servitude? By what authority do you make such detestable war against these people who were dwelling gently and peacefully in their lands, and visit death and destruction on so many of them? Why do you oppress and weaken them by denying them medicine when they are sick so that they die from the excessive work that you demand? In other words, you kill them every day to gain wealth! Are you concerned to see that someone teaches them about their God and Creator? Do you attend to having them baptized, hear Mass, observe feast days and Sundays? Are they not men? Do they not have souls? Are you not commanded to love them as yourselves? Don't you understand this? Why are you so sunk in lethargy, so fast asleep? It is certain that in your present state you have no more hope of salvation than the Moors or Turks who lack and do not want the faith of Jesus Christ.

The settlers formulated their protests and took them to the Governor, Diego Columbus, claiming that the friar was trying in a shocking manner to impugn the sovereignty of the Spanish King over the Indies which the Pope had granted. They demanded satisfaction—the expulsion of the offending priest. The quarrel was carried all the way to Ferdinand who ordered Diego Columbus to reprimand Montesinos and his brethren, warning them that persistence in their error would mean return to Spain on the first available ship "because every hour that persons of such dangerous opinions remain, they will do great harm to the interests of the island."

The order, reinforced by repetition, clearly indicated that such preaching had to stop. The rebels grew bold and sent Montesinos to Spain to defend their position even though the economic and political interests, the officials and the hierarchy had leagued against them on both sides of the ocean. That was the first rebellion of the clergy in America.

Encomenderos and slave owners confronted Montesinos with two learned men. The rich settlers chose the Franciscan Alonso del Espinal to state their case before the judge at Burgos; the affluent colonial authorities gave the same responsibility to the cosmographer and jurist, Martín Fernández de Enciso. The latter justified the oppression and despoliation of the aborigines in the name of God and the Pope, holding that "the Catholic King had the right to make them give him the land since it had been given

7

by God and by the Pope in His name and had been taken from them because they are idolaters."

As a consequence the conformist Church came also to Latin America and became powerful in the shadow of violence and the exorcism of remorse. The great church dignitaries who kept it committed to slavery and exploitation of the land and mines were quick to bless that despoliation and to castigate the dissidents without mercy. Since Queen Isabella's time, the Church in Spain had been vigilant in maintaining orthodoxy. Its implacable arm, the Inquisition of Tomás de Torquemada, the Holy Office, had purified with fires of green wood the dogma that served the powerful. In Cajamarca Fray Vicente de Valverde justified in juridical-religious formulas the execution of Atahualpa, the last Inca, thus exonerating the victors. The rebel Church of Tucumán failed to follow that example, however, when in 1581, Bishop Vitoria, at the head of the young priests, defied Governor Lerma's arbitrary actions.

In the eighteenth century three Mexican thinkers of the Society of Jesus enriched the humanist current in the Latin American Church. One was Francisco Javier Alegre, theologian, mathematician, denouncer of the traffic in Negro slaves, and author of treatises on the origin of authority who wrote that "authority is founded in the social nature of man, but its immediate source is the consent of the community." Another was the philosopher Andrés de Guevara Basoazábal who struggled "against the prejudice, which in other times had powerfully influenced many minds to the greatest detriment of learning, that modern philosophy insensibly leads to religious license and that its cultivators, consequently, willingly expose themselves to the risk of turning their backs on the Catholic religion." A third, Pedro José Márquez, held that "with respect to culture, true philosophy does not recognize incapacity in any man because he has been born white or black or because he has been reared at the poles or in the torrid zone."

Humanists of the 1700's, like Miguel Hidalgo, shaped the insurgent intellectual generation through their university positions and as writers. Among them was Father José Celestino Mutis, a native of Cádiz, a mathematician, naturalist, founder of the

Astronomical Observatory and the New Granada Botanical Expedition, who became the most important scientific force in the three and one-half centuries of the colonial period.

The humanist rebel Church and the conforming Church with its closed mind continued their divergent ways during the struggle for independence and during the republican era. On the one side were the priests who combated colonialism, including Fray Servando Teresa de Mier and Melchor de Talamantes, Miguel de Hidalgo, José María Morelos, and Mariano Matamoros in New Spain, Béjar y Muñecas in the rebellion of Cuzco in 1814, Félix Varela in Cuba, among others. On the royalist side with the forces of Calleja and General Pablo Murillo were the clergy of Bishop Manuel Abad y Queipo, who had excommunicated Hidalgo, and those of the Sacristan Juan Bautista were at the service of Morillo, "the pacificator."

The Old Church, accustomed to participation in colonial rule, resisted recognition of the new republican order of independence from Spain which the insurgents had established. It opposed José de San Martín and the *juntistas* who followed Bernardo O'Higgins in whose ranks fought some "devilish" clerics accused by the hierarchy, faithful to ancient privileges, of liberalism and of succumbing to French ideas. Francisco Miranda, Simón Bolívar, and Francisco de Paula Santander encountered belligerent, tenacious opposition from the Old Church during their campaigns of liberation and organization of the Republic of Granada. From the use of popular superstitution against the revolutionaries, as in the case of the earthquake which almost destroyed Caracas during Holy Week in 1812, to the hesitancy of Bishop Narciso Coll y Prat in his wavering loyalty to the new institutions, the monarchical clergy opposed the republican leaders.

After conforming finally with the new institutions of independence, the clergy exercised all their enticing power upon the new class of monopolists of wealth, and placed themselves on the side of the great landholders who continued in the tradition of the *encomenderos*. Bishop Clemente de Jesús Mungía exemplified in Mexico the persistent hostility of the Old Church during the Reform (1850's–1860's) to the laws designed to relieve the nation

9

of the weight of an unpopular colonial heritage. The Revolution had been inspired by the writings of a theologian of liberal ideas, the brilliant orator and writer, José María Luis Mora, who, like Hidalgo, was from Guanajuato.

Forty-six popes had occupied the seat of Peter, and 576 years had elapsed between the time of Alexander Borgia and Angel Roncalli. On becoming Pope, John XXIII undertook to revitalize the Church, to turn it toward the contemporary world, to rejuvenate it. That constituted the *aggiornamento*—the effort to bring the Church up to date. For the first time since the primitive Church of fishermen and carpenters, there was a search among Roman Catholics for the popular essence of Christianity. Achieving it in Latin America will depend on the progressive clergy, the ones who have been neglected and persecuted since the very moment of the discovery of the New World. The Old Church, now as then, is resistant to change. After more than five centuries, the struggle which began with the sermons of Fray Antonio de Montesinos in Española continues as a reality.

The following pages attempt to present the principal protagonists and episodes of the actual confrontation of the Old Church and the Young Church in Latin America, between the conformist and rebellious sectors of the clergy and laity in three important expressions of the innovations that the *aggiornamento* has proposed: the social, with the lucid and valiant Brazilian Bishop of Olinda and Recife, Helder Cámara, at its head; the scientific, personified in the wisdom and learning of the Mexican Bishop of Cuernavaca, Sergio Méndez Arceo; and the canonical, expressed in priestly defections resulting from the slowness of reform, particularly with regard to celibacy. Finally, there is an attempt to formulate a provisional balance with respect to the consequences of the revolution in the Church within the Latin American political groups of the left and the right. Also some hypotheses are proposed about the future of this internal confrontation of the two sectors of the Church which Paul VI has characterized with bitterness and surprise as a crisis.

The *Aggiornamento*

Suddenly everything changed. On October 28, 1958 the conclave of cardinals which met to elect a successor to Pius XII chose Angel Roncalli, son of an humble working-class family of Bergamo, who became John XXIII. With him the Church inaugurated a new era in its long history by evaluating the complex and dogmatic realities of the modern world in the light of its neglected origins, and by giving them new life in order to make a start in overcoming the burdensome legacies of medieval and renaissance times.

The discussion began at the top. In his encyclical, *Mater et Magistra*, the "Good Pope" aroused the dormant conscience of the Catholic world by proclaiming that "we are all responsible for the poor of the world." In that instance he was concerned not with charity nor that occasional philanthropy which purchases good consciences with second-hand tears and weeping for ladies and gentlemen of high society, but with the question of social justice based on an active and cooperative effort which would permit all to share in the fruits of production.

The hardened spirit of many in the hierarchy and the groups in power interpreted the Pope's words as a provisional, rhetorical concession to the weak. They thought he was offering provident doses of the opiate of religion to keep the masses quiet and impassive in the hope of celestial benefits seen only from afar in this "vale of tears," the rigors of which they should endure with resignation as punishment for their sins.

John XXIII directed his words to the priests in their true apostolic mission; to the priests of the afflicted. Young Latin American clergy began to reflect that as a matter of fact the doctrine of poverty is included, practically, in all the *Gospel*. The life and word of Christ were in His time, and continue to be today, disturbing to whoever makes the accumulation and enjoyment of riches the only reason for existence. A faithful image of the poor began to pervade John XXIII's documents, arousing from their pastoral lethargy the cultivated and sensitive ministers in countries weighed down by the hunger, sickness, and ignorance of the great majority of the people. Among the vast, miserable, exploited areas of the world, Latin America has been most aroused by Pope John's message. The word of Christ is still as revolutionary as it was more than two thousand years before. It continues to irritate the Pharisees and merchants and to open up horizons for the forgotten ones.

Pope John proposed an order which would liberate men from the modern slavery to capital. In *Mater et Magistra* he accepted socialization as a proper measure because it serves mankind; he declared himself in favor of the abolition of inequities and for the participation of the workers in the fruits of capital investment, and participation in the highest levels of business enterprise, and he criticized the giant economic corporations and industrial monopolies. In that encyclical he also approached the fundamental demands of socialism. In the subsequent *Pacem in Terris*, the Pope went even further by advocating the peaceful co-existence of the two ideological blocs that divide the world, and by condemning the anonimity of neo-capitalistic enterprise.

In the short four and a half years of his reign, that *pater amabilis*, "humble successor to St. Peter," as he designated himself, initiated a new era in the Church that ecclesiastical historians call the "Johnian" epoch. He let fresh air into the Church; he opened windows to our world, even doors and floodgates. "John's revolution" found expression in Vatican Council II which he conceived and prepared for the liberation of the dormant energies of the Church.

In his discourse of October 11, 1962, opening the highest assembly of the Church, John XXIII pointed out that

The greatest concern of the Ecumenical Council is this: that the sacred deposit of Christian doctrine should be guarded and taught more efficaciously. That doctrine embraces the whole of man, composed as he is of body and soul. And, since he is a pilgrim on this earth, it commands him to tend always toward heaven.

This demonstrates how our mortal life is to be ordered in such a way as to fulfill our duties as citizens of earth and of heaven, and thus to attain the aim of life as established by God. That is, all men, whether taken singly or as united in society, today have the duty of tending ceaselessly during their lifetime toward the attainment of heavenly things and to use, for this purpose only, the earthly goods, the employment of which must not prejudice their eternal happiness.*

In the same document he called attention to the Church's mission at that time and gave notice that it "must ever look to the present, to the new conditions and new forms of life introduced into the modern world which have opened new avenues to the Catholic apostolate."**

Following the death of John XXIII, June 3, 1963, the Church experienced one of the major moments of tension in its history. The wise and smiling laborer of Bergamo had constructed a wide bridge between the Church and humankind which the poor, the disinherited, and the dissident brethren of our time could cross. Even atheists such as Nicolai Podgorny, President of the Presidium of the Supreme Soviet of the USSR made an official visit to the Holy See. From that time no one could interfere with the relationship of the Church with the multitudes who daily become more numerous and more indigent or prevent their access to contemporary ideas.

A considerable number of young Latin American clerics gladly accepted John's invitation. They found that they had to break down the outmoded structures of the Church because others, disdainful and attached to the higher clergy and the privileged classes, were aware that the hierarchy, traditionally at their service, knew that only the Communists would take "those things" seriously. Nor were they wrong. *Kommunist*, an organ of the Central Committee of the Communist Party of the USSR, criticized certain Soviet authors who failed to take into account changes that had occurred in the Vatican. It stated in its edition for April, 1964,

---

*Walter M. Abbot, S.J., editor. The Very Rev. Msgr. Joseph Gallagher, translator. *Documents of Vatican II*, (New York, 1966), 713-14.
**Ibid.

"Failure to see those changes which daily become more pronounced in religious doctrine in an endeavor to achieve a renewal in new forms or to take into consideration the purpose of the Church to come out of the epoch of the 'crusades' and 'witch hunts' is to indulge in a myopia that has nothing to do with Marxism."

If the theoreticians of Russian Communism saw clearly the change of direction the Church was taking in Latin America, those Catholics clinging to the power and medieval privileges of the elite were confident that the Holy See would return to its ancient position. John's death would make it possible.

Vatican Council II

Those who took the position that Pope John's orientation was nothing more than a fleeting episode in the Church had no lack of arguments. Had not Leo XIII promulgated, May 15, 1891, the encyclical *Rerum Novarum?* How has the world changed since that Pope said that the Church was on the side of the proletariat? Leo XIII had subscribed to the doctrine of the class struggle, stating that "the violence of public disorder has divided cities into two classes of citizens, with an immense gulf lying between them. On the one side is a faction of exceedingly powerful because exceedingly rich. Since it alone has under its control every kind of work and business, it diverts to its own advantage and interest all production sources of wealth, and exerts no little power in the administration itself of the State. On the other side are the needy and helpless masses, with minds inflamed and always ready for disorder."* Who paid any attention to them? There was nothing to fear.

Few remember the reprimand Pius XI pronounced exactly forty years later in his encyclical *Quadragesimo Anno* in which he said, "This accumulation of power, the characteristic note of the modern economic order, is a natural result of limitless free com-

---

*Encyclical Letter of Pope Leo XIII, "Condition of the Working Class." New translation authorized by the Holy See. *The Encyclicals of a Century*, (Derby, New York, no date), 44–45.

petition, which permits the survival of those only who are the strongest, which often means those who fight most relentlessly, and pay least heed to the dictates of conscience."* Had not that accumulation of power and resources continued in those four decades? Only the communists tried to prevent it. Good Catholics of the time paid no attention either to Leo XIII or Pius XI. About the only ones who have listened to John XXIII are the so-called "red clergy." That was obvious.

The blindness of injustice prevents the recognition of the degree to which the teachings of the "Good Pope" have penetrated wide sectors of the Latin American priesthood and, moreover, in the most alert and sensitive areas of non-conformity.

Giovanni Batista Montini, Archbishop of Milan, a manufacturing city whose suburbs reflect in contradictions and paradoxes the dramas of the modern industrial world, was elected successor to Pope John XXIII. It is he who will decide which side the Church is on.

As a cardinal, the new Pope Paul VI attended the first part of Vatican Council II. He has studied each of its schemas and understands them well. In his first radio address to the world, June 22, 1964, he stated, "The preeminent part of our pontificate will be concerned with the continuation of Ecumenical Vatican Council II, the center of attention of all men of good will. This is the principal work on which we want to consecrate all the energies the Lord has given us, in order that the Catholic Church, which shines in the world like a flag raised over distant nations (Cfr. Isa. 5:26), can attract to itself all men with the majesty of its organization, the youthfulness of its spirit, the renewal of its structures, and the multiplicity of its forces, arising *ex omni trivu, et lingua, et populo, et natione.* (Apoc.: 5, 9). This will be the first thought of our pontifical ministry."

The documents approved by Vatican Council II conclude with a salute to rulers: "allow us to spread everywhere without hindrance the gospel of peace." To men of science: "What have our efforts

---

*Encyclical Letter of Pope Pius XI, "Social Reconstruction," Official Vatican Text. *Ibid.*, 234.

amounted to during these four years except a more attentive search for and deepening of the message of truth entrusted to the Church and an effort at more perfect docility to the spirit of truth?" To artists: "This world in which we live needs beauty in order not to sink into despair." To workers: "The Church is aware of your sufferings, your struggles, and your hopes." To the poor, the sick, to all who suffer: "Know that you are not alone, separated, abandoned, or useless."*

The Council's task of doctrinal renovation embraced the internal life of the Church and, with renewed vigor raised questions about key aspects of human existence in contemporary society. A new spirit surged from its pronouncements—the post-conciliar spirit which Latin American priests made their own, immediately being labeled "rebels." They proposed to denounce the oppression of peasants and laborers in that part of the world, and to promote the adaptation of ecclesiastical structures to those schemas.

The synthesis of the directives emanating from Vatican Council II (perhaps the most explicit evidence of the spirit that animated its deliberations and conclusions) may be found in the concepts incorporated in the document entitled "Pastoral Constitution concerning the Church in the Present World" which stated,

Never has the human race enjoyed such an abundance of wealth, resources, and economic power. Yet a huge proportion of the world's citizens is still tormented by hunger and poverty, while countless numbers suffer from total illiteracy. Never before today has man been so keenly aware of freedom, yet at the same time, new forms of social and psychological slavery make their appearance.

Although the world of today has a very vivid sense of its unity and of how one man depends on another in needful solidarity, it is most grievously torn into opposing camps by conflicting forces. For political, social, economic, racial, and ideological disputes still continue bitterly, and with them the peril of a war which would reduce everything to ashes. True, there is a growing exchange of ideas, but the very words by which key concepts are expressed take on quite different meanings in diverse ideological systems. Finally, man painstakingly searches for

The Documents of Vatican II, 730–735, *passim.*

a better world, without working with equal zeal for the betterment of his own spirit.*

The course set by the Council gave new life to Christianity which began to return to its original sources. They constituted a complete program of action in social matters that fired many Latin American priests with enthusiasm and filled them with apostolic fervor. Happy, but unprepared, they undertook to put that program into effect in their communities.

If the colossal economic power which humanity in general has at its disposition at this moment in history is manifested in hunger, misery, and ignorance for three-fourths of the inhabitants of our planet, then those fabulous riches are badly utilized and badly distributed. The rural clergy of Latin America had seen this for several centuries; parish priests in the slums know the hardships of their parishioners in the *favelas* of Brazilian cities; in the *villas miserias* of Buenos Aires, Córdoba and Rosario; in the *ranchos* of Caracas, Bogotá, Medellín, and Cali; in the *callampas* of Santiago, Arica, and Valparaíso. The highest authority of the Church in its twenty-first Council had condemned that tyranny and had called on its ministers to take up the struggle against it.

If man today searches with intense anxiety for nothing more than his freedom, the shrewd usurpers of power use technology to set up subtle systems of servitude. Every day many Latin American priests see how the means of communication are subverted, cheerfully, in a vortex of distortions that promotes the accumulation of wealth. If nothing disturbs the landed aristocracy or their affairs, the media speak of peace. They say that men belong either among the "good," the "righteous," that is, those who accept the establishment, or among the "subversives" and "enemies of order," that is, antagonists of the status-quo or non-conformists. Everything depends on vague political ideas, accepted only if they conform to the interests of the groups in power, to the economic ability of the individual, or to the color of one's skin.

As those devices have been used from the earliest times in main-

Ibid., 202–203.

taining class prejudices, the percipient clergy of Latin America were already aware of them. Now Vatican Council II had condemned them and had called on the clergy to take a firm position against discrimination on account of political ideas, poverty, or race. It had also pointed out to them that unity and interdependence on earth are subject to the definite risk of a clash between the two powers with each seeking to establish its own supremacy. The clergy should work for peace by bringing about agreement in defense of humanity and by smoothing over the irrationalities of sectarian ideology.

The ecumenical voice of the Church was speaking with a previously unknown universality. Two thousand, three hundred sixty-one cardinals, archbishops, bishops, and superiors of religious orders from all over the world, surrounded by the respect and expectations of lay observers from five continents and by representatives of separated churches, had spoken from the Basilica of St. Peter. Among the conciliar fathers were fifty-nine representatives of the billion inhabitants of the Eurasian communist bloc, voices of its sixty million Catholics. The Church had demonstrated a wish to engage in dialogue with Marxists and atheists.

The Church, universal in nature, had initiated a move to open itself to the contemporary world. It had revitalized its faith and had become receptive, thus invigorating doctrine for men of our epoch without discrimination.

Paul VI expressed the post-conciliar spirit thus formulated in *Populorum Progressio*, a spur and complement to the work of Vatican Council II which reinforced the faith and served as a deciding factor in stimulating the most sensitive, liveliest, and freshest intelligences of the Latin American clergy to undertake the search for a better life.

A Step Forward: *Populorum Progressio*

On March 26, 1967 the Vatican issued Pope Paul VI's encyclical *Populorum Progressio* which proved a disagreeable surprise for the Manicheans. He carried forward the task John XXIII had begun by pointing out the causes of exploitation and the modern ways of enslaving and degrading the weak. He indicated the sources of the poison that had envenomed commercial exchange among nations and frustrated the hopes for well-being of people in countries with façades of autonomy and freedom which, however, have been subjected to a colonial dependence that has perverted the expectation of achieving a minimum level of decent living.

For the first time in history the social doctrines of the Church attained a worldwide application. Paul VI's analysis of the injustice prevailing in the relations among nations which threatens world peace went even further than that of his predecessor in the seat of St. Peter. International economic imbalance leads to war. It determines the misery of poor countries that pay with their hunger, sicknesses, and ignorance for the affluence of highly industrial societies. The starving, unhealthy, and unlettered people of Latin America, Asia, and Africa pay tribute with the bitter reality of their destinies to the distant centers of corporate enterprise and rampant consortiums.

No mutilation of human existence is acceptable. Christ called man to a full life in all realms: spiritual, ethical, political, social, and economic. Henceforth the Church will recognize as reprehensible injustice whatever limits the scope of Catholic humanism, vivified after many centuries by John XXIII's encyclicals, developed by Vatican Council II, and started on the way to fruition by Pope Paul VI—"the Christian vocation can only be a vocation of all mankind like the Incarnate Spirit."

Permeated by this new spirit, the conscience of the Church should reject any complicity whatever with the beneficiaries of the anti-Christian situation of violence. The Church had broken the bonds that had tied it to the arrogance of one victor after another. The bitterest denunciation of those ties was expressed by Rudolph Hochhuth in *El Vicario.* Paul VI would demonstrate with *Populorum Progressio* the sincere profundity of the "Good Pope's" words, directed to the conciliar fathers, when he referred to the *aggiornamento* of the Catholic community: "We have the immense consolation of knowing that the Church, free at last of the bonds that hindered it in the past, can through us raise its solemn and majestic voice from this Vatican Basilica as from a Second Apostolic Room of the Last Supper."

The Church was cancelling its ancient compromises, recovering its autonomy, reestablishing its original freedom of thought and action. On June 3, 1967 the same year in which he issued *Populorum Progressio*, Paul VI received, in special audience at the Vatican, President Podgorny who displayed on that occasion the insignia of a "hero of the Soviet Union." On April 27 of the previous year he had received Andrei Gromyko, Minister of Foreign Relations of the USSR. On Christmas, 1964 Paul VI had said, "We recover what there is of truth and authenticity in all religion and in all human opinion for the purpose of promoting concord among peoples and the working together in good will."

Paul VI said in greeting the Soviet President, "We are very happy to receive you. Your visit is truly welcome." Podgorny replied, "I, too, am pleased." They conversed for an hour and ten minutes about the problem of achieving peace, particularly in Vietnam, and about the situation of Catholics in the Soviet Union. At the end of the interview Paul VI presented his visitor with a reproduction of a work by Leonardo da Vinci.

Less than two months later the Holy See made known the encyclical *Populorum Progressio*. Immediately the *Wall Street Journal*, the New York periodical which is the voice of the highest financial circles in the United States, characterized it as warmed-over Marxism. "If I were an integral part of the Wall Street scene, perhaps I would have the same opinion," replied Antonio Batista Fragoso, Bishop of Creatus, whose determined post-conciliar attitude provoked repression directed at him by the combined interests of the Brazilian military and magnates. Repression was aimed as well at Bishops Helder Cámara of Olinda and Recife, Waldir Calhiero of Volta Redonda, Joao Resende of Belo Horizonte, and Cándido Padía of Lorena. The extreme right believed that Paul VI was painting the Vatican red from morning to night. Those wielding power encouraged and financed the rightists, for they believed the establishment was threatened.

The progressive Brazilian Catholic hierarchy, the most advanced on social issues in Latin America, received *Populorum Progressio* as a genuine and opportune testament of truth conducive to a more just order. Bishop Fragoso himself hailed it as "an encyclical for the oppressed people of the Third World which explicitly and valiantly condemns oppression through imperialism and alienation. The Church supports the hope of liberation and stands for the individual in his dignity and his aspirations. An immense task remains for us, for all of us who claim to be Christians. Beginning with the bishops we must be prepared for an about-face, for a profound reform of society such as the Pope calls for."

Helder Cámara, Bishop of Olinda and Recife, regarded the encyclical as "a message of courage and hope." He specifically stated, "What he says about the rights of property, about liberal capitalism, justice, and peace has decisive importance in the struggle for progress. One of the gravest obstacles has been removed: those property rights which have seemed so absolute and so sacred that to touch them was tantamount to heresy. Now in *Populorum Progressio* Paul VI openly affirms that *no one has an unconditional and absolute right to private property.* He points out very clearly that *no one has the right to reserve for his exclusive use more than he needs when others lack necessities.* He proclaims, moreover, that *the earth was given to all and not merely to the rich.*"

According to José Delgado, Bishop of Fortaleza, Brazil, "The encyclical *Populorum Progressio* goes further than the four great previous social encyclicals *(Rerum Novarum, Quadragesimo Anno, Mater et Magistra,* and *Pacem in Terris)* and has a firm foundation in Vatican Council II to the degree that it heeds the legitimate longing of the people for social justice for all, Catholic and non-Catholic alike."

The analysis of the world's population presented in *Populorum Progressio* became an inescapable reality. Its bluntness aroused the wrath of the dominant elements. Paul VI revealed the Philistine character of the times—the fact that the rich were becoming richer and the poor either remaining poor or becoming poorer. The figures that the Pontiff cited were surprising. At that time, 17 per cent of the world's population consumed almost 50 per cent of the goods produced while the rest subsisted on what remained.

Why should this shocking inequity prevail? Because one country, the United States, consumes 50 per cent and controls 80 per cent of the world's riches. Paul VI attributed the poverty of some nations in part to the fact that their colonial past had retarded their development and deprived them of technical skills which resulted in delayed industrial development, monoculture in agriculture, and a variety of abuses in the national distribution of wealth. The phenomenon has already been exposed to the point of satiety. On the periphery of capitalism are the underdeveloped countries, tributaries to the system, whose economies have been deformed by an industrial neo-colonialism. That Third World of *latifundia* and monoculture, militarism and lack of education, inadequate means of communication, and physical debility which results from semi-starvation, struggles in the misery of the vicious circle imposed by the exploitation of raw materials and the impossibility of utilizing them in industry or even of producing sufficient food. For the first time the most authoritative voice in the Church had been raised in connection with this sensitive issue.

Logically, then, the revolutionary idea which had run the length and breadth of the earth was nourished by the conviction that no country or people need be poor or suffer hunger, that sufficient technical development was available to assure every human being a decent life and comfortable existence. Actually, the world's resources are not limitless. The festering resentment against misery has been expressed in the contemporary social outbursts of the underdeveloped world although poverty is not, in itself, a revolutionary factor. What happens, as in Latin America, is that when the masses understand that poverty is not inevitable and that only a few enjoy the world's goods, revolutionary expectations arise.

Populorum Progressio pointed out that Christians have the moral obligation to do everything they can to remedy the miserable, radically inhuman situation of the world's poor. Paul VI advocated a more rational distribution of wealth during the next twenty or thirty years. A system should be found that will diminish the flow of wealth into the hands of those already rich and prevent an increase in misery that oppresses those already miserable. The Supreme Pontiff indicated that we need a complete change of the economic system which now governs the finances of the world and is responsible in great part for the inequity between rich and poor. Only such a new order could eliminate the humiliating paternalism of charity. There must be a re-examination of the community in order to create economic and political structures capable of achieving radical reforms.

In Latin America the rank-and-file members of the clergy as well as the intellectuals among them welcomed Paul VI's words. For them, the encyclical was an exact diagnosis of problems they had known long and well through direct experience in cities, rural districts, and villages. They rejoiced that Pope Paul VI had continued, amplified, and had given substance to the orientation of "John XXIII's Revolution." A new atmosphere, free, open to dialogue, was established in the relations of the Church with its popular base, the multitudes of the disinherited who found the young clergy an advance guard defending their demands and looking upon them as their own. The wealthy element of the establishment in Latin America did not hide its displeasure with and fear of *Populorum Progressio*. They prepared for a struggle by allying themselves with the agents, official and unofficial, of the great international consortiums which had already vented their spite against the Supreme Pontiff.

The struggle has been hard and uneven. The clergy of the Young Church has had to face the aroused susceptibilities of the economic, social, and political beneficiaries of an unjust established order disposed to go to any lengths in defense of the status quo. They also have had to contend with the lack of pastoral understanding and the sclerotic rigidity of high-ranking ecclesiastics, with the blunderbusses who had inherited the *latifundia*, and with the new upper class of financiers. The certainty that the highest authority of the Church was on their side bolstered the morale of the Latin American clergy. The conviction prevailed that they had only to apply the conciliar decisions and follow the instructions imparted by the latest encyclicals.

Two currents produced controversy and debate within the Church. The Vatican Curia, the compact bureaucratic apparatus which surrounds the Pope, raised a curtain of incense and psalms which hindered the Holy See from hearing the clamor and learning about conditions of the unfortunate people in the Third World, especially those of Latin America. Reactionary elements among the clergy attained their first and resounding victory with the issuance of the encyclical *Humanae Vitae*.

A Step Back: *Humanae Vitae*

After five years of anticipation, on July 30, 1968 the Vatican issued the encyclical *Humanae Vitae* which Paul VI had signed four days earlier. Wordy, protracted studies and strong differences had preceded it. In October, 1963, during the *aggiornamento* John XXIII established a commission of three theologians and three laymen to decide doctrines with respect to birth control. Pope Paul VI enlarged and reinforced the commission by including married couples, sociologists, and additional theologians. In March, 1967 he expanded the body by adding seven cardinals and nine bishops, expecting that they would take into account all aspects of the issue in light of biological discoveries, and in light of the new economic and social factors that had intensified the world population problem which was becoming more critical daily.

Having sounded out public opinion the Church continued its *aggiornamento* in this area of universal interest. The following are some expressions of that opinion. In the January, 1966 Jesuit review, *Les Etudes*, Father Beiraert wrote, "It would occur to no one to designate as *artificial* in a pejorative sense the means medical science and technology use in a case of sickness to modify the natural processes of the body." In October, 1967 the World Congress of the Lay Apostolate, a sort of estates general of Catholic secularism, expressed the hope that the Church would adopt a position concerning fundamental moral and spiritual values while "leaving the choice of scientific methods of family planning to husband and wife so that they could act in accordance with their Christian faith and on the basis of medical and scientific advice." From Puerto Rico Jesuit Salvador Freixedo testified to the attitude of a sector of the Church not directly interested in the study, stating that, "We who attended the Third Congress of Laymen in

Rome could see how the nearly 3,000 people who packed the Palazzo Pio applauded frantically each time the matter of birth control was mentioned. Their loud applause clearly expressed what was in their hearts—a desire for change and for leaving the matter of conception to the free choice of husbands and wives."

The pontifical commission was divided; consequently, opposing conclusions reached Paul VI. One was prepared by the president of the commission, Cardinal Alfredo Ottaviani, Grand Master of the body formerly called the Holy Office, known for his reactionary views. Only three members agreed with him; the rest signed the other report.

The minority report absolutely proscribed every method of birth control. The majority report did not condemn artificial means of birth control—in particular, the pill. Its conclusion was simple: the problem involved a question of method in which the Church need not intervene.

Paul VI hesitated. The laxity of Catholics in the period following Vatican Council II aroused his concern. He believed with an almost obsessive fear that they were succumbing to an overwhelming desire to share in the material well-being of modern life and were losing their principles in the process. He sought in his encyclical of June 24, 1967, *Sacerdotalis Celibatus*, to restrain the tendency. A year later in the plaza of St. Peter he proclaimed the Creed with ancient formulas about the content of the faith, deliberately putting aside more recent theological investigations. He has slowed down "John XXIII's Revolution" with the same sort of concern that affected the Kremlin after the period of de-emphasizing Stalin. At the same time he was aware that when Vatican Council I had convened in 1869, world population had recently exceeded a billion, and that less than a hundred years later, when John XXIII convoked Vatican Council II, the number had tripled.

When Paul VI prepared to sign the encyclical *Humanae Vitae*, the population had increased to three and one-half billion. If the trend continues at the same rate, by the end of this century there will be seven billion inhabitants on the earth. Paul VI was aware of the fact that, even with scientific advances already achieved and with those we may expect in the immediate future, there are no means for adequately providing food, clothing and shelter, instruction, employment, and protection from sickness with reasonable tranquility and peace for such a population on our shrunken planet.

Projections of world population trends indicate that by the beginning of the next century Latin America, with an increase of one hundred million every five years, will have a greater population than the Soviet Union, and twice as many young people as the United States. That population will inundate the marketplace, choke the systems of education, and literally consume that part of the economy needed for capital development.

High ecclesiastical circles in Europe learned by 1968 that the encyclical was ready. The general nature of its intent and direction had also leaked out. The Pope had the collaboration of ten conservative Vatican theologians in its preparation. Intervention by Cardinals Leo Joseph Suenens of Belgium, Franziskus König of Austria, and Bernardus Alfrink of the Low Countries did no more than delay it for a month.

The world reacted with amazement and alarm to the contents of the encyclical *Humanae Vitae* issued on July 30, 1968. In it Paul VI forcefully condemned anything which tended to impede procreation artificially because "every marriage act must remain open to the transmission of life." He supported his determination in view that "birth control promotes conjugal infidelity and a general lowering of morals." A professor of gynecology at the Catholic University of Georgetown, D. André Hellegers, deplored this statement as a "gratuitous slap at Protestant wives." The encyclical further made an appeal to the governments of the world to proscribe the means for birth control. It anticipated the tempests of protest against the Pope's decision, and emphasized that "This teaching will perhaps not be easily received by all. . . . In defending conjugal morals in their integral wholeness the Church knows she contributes toward the establishment of a truly human civilization."*

---

*Quotations from *Humanae Vitae* in these paragraphs are from the Encyclical Letter of His Holiness Pope Paul VI, "On the Regulation of Birth." July 29, 1968. Official translation. (Boston, no date), *passim*.

The Supreme Pontiff was not mistaken. Immediately the encyclical met with a deluge of criticisms and protests revealing a marked aspect of frank hostility toward the Vatican. The Swiss theologian Hans Küng declared that the Pope was mistaken and that the encyclical could become a new Galileo case. John McKenzie, a Jesuit at Notre Dame University and an erudite biblical scholar, believed that "With this pronouncement concerning birth control the papacy has lost its leadership, and even if it should be able to recover it, it would take two hundred years."

Not only did this encyclical leave *Populorum Progressio* practically without foundation, it contradicted it. *Humanae Vitae* was promulgated just twenty days before Paul VI's departure for Colombia, a country located in one of the most underdeveloped areas of the world with a demographic growth rate of three per cent annually. As a result there are too many children for each adult, each teacher, each doctor, each house, each cemetery, each rudimentary industry, and even for each priest. The annual rate of increase in the rest of the world in scarcely two per cent. On the same day that the encyclical was issued, Hernán Mendoza Hoyos, head of the Division of Population Studies in Colombia, the country preparing to receive Paul VI with devotion and jubilation, declared that it would not affect Colombia's official programs for restraining the population explosion. He stated that 370,000 contraceptive units were being sold per year, and that the quantity would increase, notwithstanding the text of the encyclical. By way of contrast, it has become known that in Chile twenty-seven per cent of blood available in blood banks is used in transfusions for victims of botched abortions.

Shortly before the first anniversary of the promulgation of *Humanae Vitae*, a congress of Colombian bishops declared that in the face of the grave situation, they were abandoning their position of an unequivocal "no" to the "pill" and would defend the *positive aspects* of the encyclical, thus tacitly acknowledging that it had some negative aspects.

The matter could not be ignored. On opening the joint meeting of the International Monetary Fund and the World Bank in Washington on September 29, 1969, Robert S. McNamara, its presi-

27

dent, considered it opportune to reiterate before more than two thousand delegates the opinion he had expressed in Buenos Aires the year before at the Interamerican Press Society gathering. Mr. McNamara, a former secretary of defense under President Kennedy and a man regarded among the most eminent in the United States, had emphasized on that occasion the urgency of family planning in Latin America, and had announced that the World Bank, as an agency for development, would give priority to the problem and would request governments seeking its aid to adopt a firm strategy for stabilization of demographic growth in their regions. *Humanae Vitae* found its counterpoint in this "encyclical" by McNamara. Again a year later, the president of the World Bank stressed in his speech in Washington the fact that population growth constitutes an important obstacle to economic and social progress among nations of the world.

Hours later the permanent commission of the Colombian Episcopal Conference with Bishop Aníbal Muñoz Duque, apostolic administrator of Bogotá, presiding, issued a fourteen-point document rejecting McNamara's position in these words, "The restriction of births among our people which is planned and financed from abroad is an affront to our independence. International pressure in the economic collaboration between underdeveloped countries and those already on the road to development has forced them to accept intense and indiscriminate birth control programs which violate the sacred consciences of individuals." Bishop Muñoz Duque gave slight attention to the many seething problems arising from the population explosion. He affirmed that "The interpretation of authentic natural law and defense of the individual's rights pertain to the authority of the Church as its exclusive and indubitable duty." After the issuance of *Humanae Vitae* he stated, covering himself with pontifical infallibility, that for Catholics "no ambiguities remain concerning the proper manner of formulating conscience and ordering its procedures in accordance with the moral law proclaimed in that encyclical within a total view of man."

Between theology and the requirements of modern technology some Latin American countries are in a dilemma. Ought they accept McNamara's "encyclical" in order to finance, to some degree, their modest plans for development, or should they accept the prohibition of Paul VI's encyclical in order to avoid internal political problems? Between the faith of workers and the prognostication of cybernetics, between idolatry of external human forms and science, such governments become involved in controversy through an ambivalent attitude toward their immediate requirements. Stimulating development of their countries to achieve satisfactions according to expectations of technocrats will arouse the fiery rancor of sacristans and bigots. Assurance to the Old Church that the problem belongs to it alone will prevent activation of any plan of development capable of satisfying within a decade the accumulation of needs that press upon a population grown out of all proportion to economic resources, natural and technical, of the countries of the Third World. Apparently the well-being of the coming generations of Latin Americans is taken lightly. Is there any possibility of the scientific foresight which supports McNamara's position?

The government of the United States is not alone in making plans for preventing runaway population growth. Evidence of the need for controlling the huge increase in population in the Third World comes from international organizations not vulnerable to the accusation of perverse imperialistic designs discerned by some in Washington's insistence—disregarding the fact that the United States makes the same effort itself. At the biennial assembly of the Food and Agricultural Organization (FAO) of the United Nations in Rome, November, 1969, its Director General, Addeke H. Boerma of the Netherlands, said that within twenty years there would be more than a billion more mouths to feed—without counting the Chinese. For some time the FAO had been reiterating its position and its alarm. According to its report of September, 1969, the problem of hunger is related to making the most advantageous use of land and sea. There is land enough for only three hectares of "living space for each man, woman, and child of our generation. Of that amount scarcely .45 of a hectare is under cultivation, and another 1.07 hectares is suitable for cultivation while of the remainder, .51 of a hectare is too mountainous and 1.01 hectares are too cold for agriculture." Boerma declared, May,

1969, that "The food crisis is worldwide and affects the most advanced countries as well as the poor ones."

What about scientific progress, ask the technocrats of demagoguery and the professional optimists. "Science," in the opinion of the Director of FAO, "will not in the near future reduce the difference between the rate of population growth and that of increase of food production." That agency's most recent statistics demonstrate that underdeveloped countries are not succeeding in feeding their people. According to those data world food production inceased about three per cent in 1968, scarcely more than the rate of increase in population. Production actually decreased, or increased at a lower rate, in regions where the need for food is greatest: in Latin America, Asia, and Africa. Except in Argentina and Uruguay, Latin Americans have marginal diets. The predictions that formed part of the material for study by the assembly of the FAO in Rome in October, 1969, indicated that the problem of unemployment for a population which will exceed 1,400,000,-000 by 1995 will be a much greater one than that of feeding them. It noted further that "not only will more human suffering accompany this problem but also more social disturbances and political instability. . . . Already there are more people on the farms than are really needed, and the problem will become more acute with technological advances in poor countries."

Josué de Castro, the world's greatest authority on "the geography of hunger," wrote for *La Pléyade* of Paris that "In 1952, the FAO came to the conclusion, following its second inquiry on feeding the world, that 60 per cent of the population had available only 2,200 calories a day; that is to say, nearly two-thirds of humanity suffered from an inadequate diet."

The Vatican showed itself impenetrable and inflexible in the face of the dissensions which *Humanae Vitae* provoked in the Catholic world. Paul VI personally supported Cardinal Patrick O'Boyle, Bishop of Washington, in a dispute with fifty priests of his diocese who had held that married persons could follow the dictates of their consciences with respect to birth control. When O'Boyle suspended them from the exercise of their ministerial functions, Paul VI supported him, intervening for the first time in a local dispute.

The Vatican remained forceful and unwavering in the position it had taken in *Humanae Vitae*. On the first anniversary of its publication, *L'Osservatore Romano* declared that whoever opposed the encyclical "is not a son of the Church." In out-of-date language of the pre-conciliar Old Church, the article came from the Congregation for the Propagation of the Faith (formerly the Holy Office) which was engaged in frustrating the *aggiornamento* in its different trends. Father Ermenegildo Lio, an Italian Franciscan friar who served as theological consultant of the congregation in charge of doctrinal discipline, signed it.

The former Holy Office through Father Lio's agency went to an extreme in affirming in the Vatican's official organ that the prohibitions of *Humanae Vitae* could not be revised by future popes. Not only did it propose to close the dialogue of the Church with priesthood and laity, but with the future. In a fervid exaltation of pontifical authority, the theologians of the Inquisition (Holy Office) confused the binding character of the Pope's voice when he speaks *ex cathedra* and establishes a doctrine with that, when he, like any other person, formulates a judgment in which he may be mistaken, that is to say, "fallible." In accordance with the doctrine of papal infallibility, a doctrine scarcely a hundred years old within the two thousand-year span of the Church's history, three conditions are necessary before a pronouncement can be designated *ex cathedra*, or what amounts to the same thing, that a papal pronouncement is infallible. The conditions are: that the Pope speak as pastor and teacher of all Christians and not as a private person; that he define a truth or doctrine that pertains to the Revelation—truths which the Holy Spirit transmits to men through the intermediation of His Vicar on Earth; and that the doctrine in question applies to the universal Church.

In accordance with the etymology of the word, encyclicals are simply circular letters. They correspond to documents known as pastoral letters to be read before congregations of the faithful. Encyclicals do not incorporate pronouncements *ex cathedra,* manifestations of the infallible authority of the Supreme Pontiff. Their modest purpose is to guard the security of doctrine. To hold that *Humanae Vitae* has the force of a pronouncement *ex cathedra* is to carry the cult of papal personality to limits incompatible with

Catholic theology, and, even more emphatically, to a point contrary to the realities of our time.

That issue is once more the core of contemporary agitation in the Church. Justifiably and urgently, means must be found to solve the problem of communication which the Young Church of Europe and America has raised. Its most brilliant theoretician is the Belgian cardinal, Leo Joseph Suenens. The revived monarchical structure of the Church has been untiring in magnifying papal infallibility. The issue is not the Pope's spiritual authority, but the matter of bringing it back to its original limits, those which it had in the democratic, austere, humanized, original Church. Cardinal Suenens' orthodox efforts clashed with bureaucratic bad habits and with arbitrary distortions converted into articles of faith by the Roman Curia represented in the dispute by Cardinal Danielou.

The Extraordinary Synod of Bishops which Paul VI convoked in October, 1969, sought an eclectic solution which might be achieved in the next few years insofar as the anachronistic rigidity of the Holy Office will permit. Its Director, Cardinal Franjo Seper of Yugoslavia, presided over the commission of thirty theologians from eighteen countries charged with examining the agenda of the Synod.

Coinciding with the Extraordinary Synod of Bishops, an European Assembly of Priests (nicknamed the Shadow-Synod by the Italian press) brought together in Rome some two hundred European priests representing more than four thousand of the clergy, along with observers from Mexico, Venezuela, Colombia, and the Dominican Republic. Its revolutionary efforts became another example of the ecumenical non-conformity which was agitating the Church. European priests in July, 1969, in Chur, Switzerland, had already obtained a wider audience among the faithful of that continent than the European episcopate had achieved during its assembly in that Swiss town, foreshadowing the simultaneous confrontation the young priests would present in Rome. Discussion of the supremely important matter of the extension of papal authority, which John XXIII had raised and Vatican Council II had wisely directed, has continued. The encyclical *Humanae Vitae* reopened the issue in countries of the Third World.

A few days before the confirmation of *Humanae Vitae* appeared in *L'Osservatore Romano*, Washington expressed its point of view in the matter in technical and sober language. The document, issued by the former Holy Office confirming Paul VI's encyclical, contrary to Catholic theology, may be interpreted as the Vatican's reply to the United States government. President Nixon's message to Congress, July 18, 1969, stated that he planned to provide free information concerning birth control to women of child-bearing age in the United States, especially to those in low-income brackets, for at the current rate, "by the year 2000, . . . there will be more than 300 million" people in the United States, an increase of 100 million in about thirty years. The chief of state of the world's richest country added that, on account of demographic increase, "if we were to accommodate the full 100 million persons in new communities, we would have to build a new city of 250,000 persons each month from now to the end of the century." According to the White House, "If present trends continue until the year 2000, the world population, now about 3,500,000,000, will double, and "the eighth billion would be added in only five years." In Nixon's view, that rate of increase creates special problems for developing nations where the population increase is greatest. He added that observers agree that the issues can be met only if there is a great deal of advance planning.

Why has the Vatican failed to take into account such a dramatic and well-known fact? Why has it clung to a thesis which if accepted will cause tremendous damage to humanity? Why has the Holy See not accepted the co-responsibility of the modern Church, a basic tenet of the *aggiornamento*? Belgian Catholic intellectuals answered with a communication to their bishops in which they said, "When the encyclical tries to establish firmly the obligatory force of the thesis, without regard to rational argument, it unavoidably raises reservations and makes any dialogue practically impossible."

The Young Latin American Church made itself heard also. Three weeks before his arrival for the first time in a country of the Third World, Paul VI had taken an action which slowed up the *aggiornamento*. Discord spread among Catholics, and the division between the two sectors of the priesthood deepened. The first Latin American protest originated in the precincts of the Cathedral of Santiago in Chile, occupied by two hundred parishioners, among whom were five priests and two nuns, seeking to move toward a democratization of the Catholic Church in Chile and in the world. They pointed out that, "The Church proclaims freedom of conscience in the matter of birth control, but by rejecting all feasible methods makes it impossible to exercise that right."

Why Do You Come, Brother Paul?

During a general audience before thousands of pilgrims in the Basilica of St. Peter, May 8, 1968, Paul VI announced his projected trip to Colombia. It would be the first time in the history of the Church that a Pope had visited Latin America, home of the most numerous and most devoted among the peoples under his influence. At the conclusion of Vatican Council II, Pope Paul VI had surprised the world with the announcement that he would go as a pilgrim to the Holy Land. Pope John XXIII had left Rome only to go to pray at Loretto and Assisi. Now Paul VI was putting himself in direct communication with the world. He would be the first pope to travel outside of Italy since Pius VII was obliged to go to Paris to crown Napoleon.

The journey announced at the Basilica of St. Peter would be the sixth of Paul VI's pontificate. He made a pilgrimage to Jerusalem in January, 1964; he arrived in India in December of the same year; he spoke before the United Nations in New York, October, 1965; in May, 1967, at Fatima, Portugal, he greeted Lucia, the only survivor of the three little Portuguese country girls who witnessed the miracle; the following day he flew to Istanbul, Turkey where he greeted the Patriarch Athenagoras. Then he announced his projected journey to Latin America, the region of the world most devoted to his authority.

Undoubtedly Paul VI knew the situation he would encounter there, especially in the country where he would manifest his affection for millions of the faithful, inhabitants of a fabulous land that extends from the Mexican bank of the Rio Grande to the Argentinian Patagonia. Something must have filtered through the thick curtain which the Roman Curia and high Latin American ecclesiastical authorities of the Old Church had drawn between the Supreme Pontiff and the almost three hundred million devoted believers. Hence Paul VI concluded his announcement in St. Peter's Basilica by noting that the next religious affirmation would be celebrated "in that Latin America where we are so loved by the multitudes of the poor and the humble who await a new and provident social justice, for peace and Christian prosperity in that immense world." Would it really be the Church of the poor, of the humble, that Paul VI would see and hear in Colombia? Would the collusion of those interested in hiding bitter truths be able to prevent his doing so?

Anxiety spread among numerous sensitive groups in Latin America, headed resolutely and firmly in each country by constantly increasing numbers of young priests who followed the post-conciliar line.

The first reaction appeared in Argentina only ten days after Paul VI's announcement. The Catholic organization, *Encuentro Latinoamericano Camilo Torres*, made up of both clergy and laity with headquarters in Buenos Aires, issued an open letter to Paul VI expressing the suspicion that "the Pope will be separated from the masses of the people; will be cut off and encircled by those opposed to the masses," and that his return to the Vatican would leave clear the implication that at Bogotá he had "played into the hands of the assassins of the workers and peasants and the exploiters of the people." The message concluded with the affirmation that the journey of the Supreme Pontiff would be used, contrary to the Pope's will, "to consolidate social injustice, oppression of the helpless, and the delivery of wealth to imperialism."

The suspicion grew rapidly that the pontifical journey would accrue to the advantage of special economic, social, and political interests by securing from Paul VI a blessing on the social injustice which enriched them.

"Brother Paul, if you do not come to commit yourself to the cause of those who struggle; if you come to consecrate the existing order, then, Brother Paul, it is better for you not to come." That was the laconic message which the young clergy of Uruguay directed to the Vatican. Those few words brought to a focus the anguish of the southern progressive clergy. It was the expression of those who desired with militant candor that the Church break the ties binding it to the ancient structures which for centuries have kept Latin America subjected to suffocating interests.

The announcement of Paul VI's visit stimulated the conscience of the continent. Minority groups, who were traditional holders of political power tied in with large landholdings and business, prepared to give Paul VI an enthusiastic, fervent welcome. They were accustomed to seeing the Church through its high officials ready to justify ancient methods of exploitation of the classes who were every day becoming more helpless. To them, the Pope is the highest authority of that apparatus that had always given its blessing to the affluence of the few, even to identifying with them in pastoral practice, the liturgy, and vesture. This was the source of the fear that perturbed and agitated the young, progressive clergy. Would Paul VI be used to justify those opprobrious social conditions against which the masses of the whole continent were rebelling?

The Pope was due to arrive in Bogotá August 21. Ten days before his arrival about two hundred Catholic clergy and laymen assembled in the Cathedral of Santiago in Chile to express their discontent with the Old Church and to state their opposition to the way that plans for the Pope's visit to America were developing. Masses in the Cathedral were suspended that Sunday. The speaker for the group, Father Andrés Opaso, one of the eight priests (three of whom did not enter the Cathedral) leading the protest, explained in the name of the occupants of the Cathedral, "We are not against the Pope or his visit. We are against the way the journey is being planned. The Church is today an aristocratic organization. It must understand the actual conditions and the daily problems of the poor." Hours later, from the interior of the Cathedral, the demonstrators made public a declaration in which they indicated that they wanted the Church to become the hearth-symbol of the Christian family; they wanted it to unite workers, students, and professionals; to become again a Church of the people "instead of a Church which is the slave to structures of social compromise; yes, a free Church which is a servant for mankind, not one allied with wealth and power." With reference to the Eucharistic Congress of Bogotá, the opening of which Paul VI would attend, they reasoned, "Christ did not need multitudes singing in the streets and acclaiming his vicarate, nor thousands of wax candles, nor beautiful altars. Christ, present among the poor needs action by those who believe in him. Christ needs support so that the exploitation of the Latin American masses may be stopped. That Congress [in Bogotá] will serve only to put into a deeper sleep those who are already sleeping." They added, "A new Church, a silent Church, seems to be rising up now among those who have faith in the Gospel but do not feel themselves always represented by ecclesiastical authority in the structure of the Church."

The two hundred who had become adherents of the Silent Church of Latin America made clear that they had occupied the Cathedral of Santiago to call the world's attention, and especially the attention of Latin America, to the distortions which threatened Paul VI's visit. They cited for support St. Gregory the Great who said, "If scandal comes because of truth, then it is better that the scandal be born than the truth sacrificed."

They sought to disinter the living origins of Christianity, founded and practiced by poor people, fishermen enlightened by the favorable example of the Maccabees, accustomed to struggle against slavery. The Church, seeking to return to the humble, must seek the way of simplicity. It should follow the practices that the first Christians established. It should not use the incomprehensible languages and cabalistic signs, but should speak in the people's own idiom, in unadorned form. That was how the Sadducees were offended. The impulses, the inspiration of the primitive Church had been suffocated from the first moment among the Latin American clergy. Now they had recovered their voices. They were awakened.

On Thursday, August 22, Paul VI alighted from the plane which had brought him from the Fiumicino Airport. As he knelt to kiss the Colombian earth, a wave of religious fervor welled up which accompanied him triumphally during the 57 hours and 40 minutes of his stay in Latin America. The venerated pilgrim in white robes was acclaimed deliriously in the precincts of the Bogotá Cathedral. When he appeared on the balcony of the cardinal's palace, along the 230 kilometers of his automobile drive, and at the descent from the helicopter from which he viewed the placid landscape of the Andean *meseta*, he saw only triumphant multitudes, bathed and disinfected for the occasion.

No one supposed that Paul's visit enriched his knowledge of the misery, hunger, ignorance, and sickness that afflict the countries of the Third World. Nor in this specially arranged scenario was the position of the Church, oscillating as it was between *Populorum Progressio* and *Humanae Vitae*, defined. Will the "Revolution of John XXIII," the *aggiornamento*, the identification with those who suffer, be continued? Or is it a matter of a tacit armistice between the Church and those who cause the increasing misery of the Latin American poor?

To some observers, Paul VI's journey to Latin America did not appear to be what the Young Church had hoped for. Analysts interpreted it as almost a consecration of the Old Church; at most, it was interpreted as an effort of Paul VI in favor of the eclectic Church. Ecclesiastic commentaries of the sector that felt victorious explained that the Church is eternal; hence the Holy See is not in a hurry.

The Social *Aggiornamento*

In The Quadrilateral Of Hunger

Brazil is probably the most obvious among the tragic paradoxes of Latin American development. It strives to reconcile in its immense territory two societies which have little in common. The people in the states of Rio de Janiero, Guanabara, and São Paulo with their industrial centers enjoy a distinctly advantageous situation in comparison with the people of the northeastern states.

The state of San Salvador marks the geographic division between the Atlantic slope and the Brazilian shield, and marks as well the division in the social and economic levels of the country. To the south, gay with the joyousness of the *samba,* dwell the *cariocas, paulistas,* citizens of Niteroi, and those who live in the rich Belo Horizonte area who enjoy fireplaces, coffee, and the prodigious deeds of soccer teams. To the northeast, in the quadrilateral of hunger, misery incubates sickness and desperation, its claws clutching the people in the states of Bahia, Sergipe, Pernambuco, Paraíba, Rio Grande do Norte, part of Ceará and Alagoas, not to mention the millions in Amazonas north of Mato Grosso.

During the tropical winter rainy season, mud covers the thorny plants and thistle of the *catingas.* The Northeast, a semi-desert region the rest of the year, becomes a slimy, unhealthy swamp. Once the torrential rains cease, the only green areas are the narrow strips of land belonging to the *latifundistas* where sugar cane and palms grow. The rest is flat, arid, miserable. Each year peasants by the thousands migrate to Minas Gerais and Mato Grosso or go to increase the *favelas* of São Paulo, Rio de Janeiro, and Niteroi. They are snared by dealers in manual laborers who deliver them as virtual slaves to the great landholders. Debts contracted in stores of the *fundos* and starvation wages mortgage their lives. The ones who manage to return to their home states are sunk in deepest misery. A considerable number remain in the slums of the great cities, brooding over their misfortunes and contemplating revenge.

Celso Furtado, the most consistent of Brazilian economists, recognizes that

to the degree that industrial development took the place of coffee economy (in the center and southern part of the country), the trend toward concentration of industrial income became relatively acute. Thus between 1948 and 1955, the contribution of the State of São Paulo to industrial income rose from 39.9% to 45.3% of the total. During the same period, that of the Northeast with twice the population of São Paulo declined from 16.3% to 9.3% of the total. In considering these trends, it is necessary to take into account the marked difference in the per capita levels of income in the two regions. Income in the Northeast is slightly less than one-fourth that of São Paulo.

The trend Celso Furtado noted in 1955 intensified during the following fourteen years. It would be difficult for the consequences of this internal inequality to appear more gloomy than they do now.

In his *Política da Fome,* Josué de Castro's objective investigation enabled him to incorporate in one datum the penury of the Northeast, a region of *latifundia* devoted to sugar cane monoculture. He pointed out that, according to an investigation carried out before World War II, the average daily food consumption there was only 1700 calories. That figure revealed the horrifying fact that millions were living in hunger. In normal biological conditions the human organism requires about 3,000 calories daily. Researchers concerned with the problem of the Brazilian northeast concur that it is becoming more serious.

The masses in the quadrilateral of hunger struggle in the corrupting depression of a subhuman level of life. Their lassitude is far from being a sought-for, placid existence. Their unwillingness to exert themselves results from and is associated with the system of exploitation of labor and low wages. For a large group there is increasing unemployment or part-time employment. Along with pauperism, the *latifundia* system cultivates a grave apathy resulting from lack of education and poor health, promiscuity and disruption of family life, irregular and inadequate diet, and congenital defects in children. The diagnosis is horrifying. Bad nutrition during infancy and school years results almost invariably in irreparable brain deterioration with its catalog of grave consequences—psychic limitations, serious physical defects, progressive diminution in the stature of children and adolescents.

Any remedy for a situation, which few have viewed with anger or even sorrow, has been left by tacit agreement among its beneficiaries and international bodies to the alchemy of statistics which knowledgeable economists (bureaucratically complacent by habit) manipulate so that their formulas will be forgotten. In this environment, a man from an affluent family, one whose hands were unmarked by toil, raised his cultivated voice with a fighting apostolic will and humane clarity forcibly to condemn the existing oppression. Helder Cámara brought up to date and illuminated after more than three and one-half centuries the person of another Brazilian, Father Antonio de Vieyra, who had come with his parents "to better their fortune in that source of riches." During the seventeenth century Vieyra struggled against the abominable abuses of those hungry for gold. He held the place in his country that Bartolomé de las Casas did in the rest of Latin America.

Helder Cámara defended the rights of the humble and excoriated the misery decreed by great landholders and the government. He spoke of development in humane and vigorous language; he called attention to the urgency of "a structural revolution" and the necessity for being alert so that "poverty will not degenerate into misery, because misery is repellent and debasing; it wounds the image of God which is in every man; it violates the right and duty of the human being with respect to his totality."

First in the northeast, his voice gave renewed hope to his oppressed compatriots and aroused great ill-will among the oppressors. Then it reached beyond the social ambience of Latin America to become the doctrine and emblem of the dissidence of the exploited and a matter of concern to the magnates. Today this Brazilian priest's protests and teachings overflow continental limits, giving direction to the exploited masses of the Third World. He has become the most valorous, intelligent, and faithful proponent of "John XXIII's Revolution."

The mighty who preside over the misfortunes of the people here and elsewhere tried to silence him. They accused him to the Pope of being subversive and applied for his transfer. Later, they begged the Pope to silence him. Professional assassins were hired to kill him; then his enemies resorted to anti-Communist organizations to make attempts on his life and the lives of ecclesiastics helping him. Will the Vatican agree to silence him?

Helder Cámara, Bishop of Olinda and Recife, is today [1969] the most illustrious person—the most closely watched and threatened in Latin America. He incarnates the Young Church with his MEB (*Movimento Educativo de Base*—Basic Educational Movement) headed by the active and intelligent Marina Bandeira. That organization attempts to promote the development of communities and to give elementary instruction in community action. The military dictatorship and the economic monopolists considered such activities and those carried on by the JOC (*Juventud Obrera Cristiana*—Christian Youth Work) so subversive that the directors have been persecuted and imprisoned.

In 1931, when he was twenty-two years old, Helder Cámara had been ordained. Thirty-three years later Paul VI named him bishop of the most important diocese in Brazil. The Vatican had rewarded him for the way he had performed his pastoral duties and for his work in the Secretariat of the Episcopal Conference of his country. He gave direction to the social *aggiornamento* of the Latin American Church. His example was a pattern to continental clergy, and his teachings were heard by millions of peasants and workers throughout the underdeveloped countries of Latin America, Asia, and Africa.

Helder Cámara convoked a meeting of Brazilian bishops at Recife in 1966. The assembly adopted a memorial concerning the grievances of the laborers of the northeast. The situation was so desperate that it induced the Bishop of Santo André, Jorge

Marcos, to proclaim the justice and necessity of armed struggle, for "imperialism and Christianity cannot coexist." Those present at the assembly agreed that

limitless ambition and boundless selfishness have created the present situation in which the poor are sacrificed for the benefit of the privileged. . . . They refuse to recognize rights acquired through labor legislation, and they take advantage of a system of justice which is slow or excessively complacent. We have seen people, oppressed by hunger and misery, give up their rights, their freedom, and their security in exchange for some small sums of money. For example, medical and hospital assistance may be promised the workers if they will give up their union activities.

Not a single newspaper was willing to publish the conclusions of the Council of Recife which they considered subversive, inspired by Marxism. Helder Cámara became known as the "Red Bishop."

Three days before Paul VI's arrival in Latin America, Helder Cámara attended the opening in Joao Pessoa of the Institute of Regional Development which had the duty of investigating and finding solutions for the geo-economic inequalities in Brazil. That occasion allowed him the opportunity for a precise statement of his social and political thought. He attributed the marginal situation of the Latin American people and other countries of the Third World which remain on the periphery of economic, political, social, and religious activities to capitalist and communist imperialism. With reference to Latin America, he reiterated his accusation that "small groups of privileged persons continue to employ violence in order to maintain their positions based on the misery of millions."

Not many hours later in Bogotá, with the Pope only a few yards away, Helder Cámara expressed his conviction that "a modification of Latin American structures are necessary. The masses must be integrated fully into economic, social, and political life instead of being left outside."

The Brazilian Bishop did not formulate a strategy for a war to liberate the masses. An objective evaluation of the Latin American situation at that point reveals that conditions were not suitable for violent solutions. In the Bishop's opinion, "any liberating war which might be declared anywhere in Latin America would be immediately suppressed by imperialist forces." In the Colombian capital, in sight of Paul VI, he made his point clearly, saying, "A bloody revolution would degenerate into an imperialistic intervention by the United States. There would be an imperialistic war against a war for liberation, because the United States would not allow a second Cuba."

In Joao Pessoa he had pointed out to the Utopians that "they should not fool themselves, because other imperialist forces would come and transform us into another Vietnam." Helder Cámara did not propose violence, but he declared, "Neither do I ask the people to fold their arms in the face of the situation." In Father Camilo Torres' country, in the presence of those who had been his scourges, and before the Supreme Pontiff, he stated, "I respect those who choose violence." In that same place he added, "Intellectuals will not make a revolution, nor politicians, nor the clergy, nor students, but the oppressed masses will; otherwise there will be no revolution." Do those oppressed masses need a precursor to awaken their consciousness, as Helder Cámara was doing, and then a leader to direct them? The Brazilian Bishop had his own ideas about that.

His strategy of resistance to oppression, his tactic for success in changing structures, arose from a profound democratic conviction which led him to believe in the popular capacity for a pacific struggle. "We must organize ourselves," he instructed those present at the Institute for Regional Development at Joao Pessoa, "in order to exert moral, liberating pressure, stemming from the principles of human rights proclaimed by the United Nations. We are going to exert pressure so that there will be no form of servility; we shall mobilize public opinion to aid the masses to become a people defending their right to life in freedom and security." He did not propose the *satyagraha,* the Gandhian type of passive resistance, but an active, massive resistance that would not resort to physical violence because of the obvious impossibility for the oppressed to emerge victorious from an armed confrontation with the repressive forces supported by the United States imperialism.

On that same occasion Bishop Helder Cámara censured the Brazilian government for lack of courage in failing to carry out agrarian reform in the northeast and affirmed that "the way in which the industrialization of that region is being achieved will not resolve the social problem."

The sectors of society which felt threatened by Helder Cámara's post-conciliar rebellion united in a chorus of direct insults, abuse, and calumnies in an attempt to frighten him, silence him, and diminish the influence of his ideas. They branded him a demagogue, labeled him the "Red Bishop," and accused him of being a subversive and a Communist. Helder Cámara knew that Antonio de Vieyra had been called a liberal, free-thinker, and enemy of the King for condemning the *entradas* into the back country to capture and enslave Indians whom they carried into forced labor on the littoral. Antonio de Vieyra had been imprisoned in 1684 for promoting the revolt in Marañón against the hunger-causing monopoly of the merchants.

After returning to his apostolic see from Colombia, Helder Cámara declared in Rio de Janeiro that reforms for bettering the conditions of the poor of the continent were near. He thought he could discern that possibility in the conclusions of the Episcopal Conference of Latin America which Paul VI had inaugurated in Bogotá. The progressive Bishop optimistically stated that "the reforms will be carried out whether or not our adversaries like it, because the entire hierarchy of Latin America through the Episcopal Conference and with the support of the Pope made a decision of that nature."

He did not feel alone nor was he intimidated. "Whoever denounces me as subversive from now on will have to extend that accusation to the entire American Church." Furthermore, "if what goes against order in the present Latin American situation is subversive, then those who desire social change are not subversives, but those who oppose it are, for that means the existence of *established disorder.*"

Early in December, 1968, the National Conference of Bishops

of Brazil met in Rio de Janeiro with about twenty-five dignitaries, predominantly centrists, attending. The body announced that "the demand for change which proposes transformation of an economic, political, social, and cultural order manifestly unjust should not be considered subversive."

How well founded was the optimism of Father Vieyra's successor? Before the Latin American Episcopal Conference, the 220 Brazilian bishops had met to make preparations for the meeting in Colombia with the theme, "The Mission of the Church in Present Day Brazil." The moderate group led by Angelo Rossi obtained 151 votes, the reformists led by Helder Cámara received 54 votes, and the traditionalists under Bishops Sigaud and Castro Maier, received 15, approximately the composition of the groups in the assembly that Paul VI had opened in Latin America.

Helder Cámara's fervent convictions sustained him in the struggle. In his opinion each human organization is divided according to its social interests more or less in the following proportions: about fifteen per cent committed to the existing unjust order, about seventy per cent with no great courage or special fervor, and, happily, a superior fifteen per cent composing a minority of admirable and audacious people. Helder Cámara thought those terms pretentious and preferred to call the minority the "followers of Abraham," father of the faith, for they continued to hope when there seemed to be no reason to hope. His benevolent wisdom led him to look for them "in every country, in every group of human beings," and to dream "of an alliance of these minorities, the followers of Abraham, from developed and underdeveloped countries, from capitalist and from socialist countries."

A reply was not long in coming. On November 24, 1968, the Secretary of Public Security of the state of Guanabara, General Luiz Franca, issued a detention order against the Bishop of Creatus, Antonio Batista Fragoso. The government alleged that letters from the prelate had been found in an apartment which had served as a base for a terrorist cell with Peking connections. The following day machine gun bullets rattled against the walls of Helder Cámara's residence already marred the previous week with offensive epithets. It was the third attack upon him.

His zeal did not slacken. At Harvard University he charged that the United States was responsible for the expansion of guerilla activities in Latin America. In his view, such groups do not constitute "signs of hope, but simply expressions of the expansionist threat of socialist rule." In New York in the confines of the Conference on Catholic Inter-American Cooperation, he outlined a new *aggiornamento* for the Latin American Church. "Our sister Cuba," he affirmed, "must be reintegrated into our community with the respect due her for her political option and acceptance of her sovereignty as a nation."

The military dictatorship, in a noisy exchange with their excellencies, let loose a persecution of the Young Church made up of the minority Abrahamites, progressive priests, students, intellectuals, and artists. On December 3, 1968, three French priests, Michel, François, and Hervé, and a Brazilian, José Geraldo, were arrested in Belo Horizonte on the accusation that they had inspired the movement known as *"Acción Popular"* which, according to the police, was infiltrated by Communists. *O Diario,* the Latin American Catholic periodical with the largest circulation, pointed out that the arrests were "a threat not only to the Church but to the people who could not rely on support by the power structure. The dominant power supports and even respects the Church and uses it when it serves its interests and tolerates its opposition and its presence until the Church becomes a threat to the regimen of injustice." Police in Belo Horizonte took some nuns as hostages when they were unable to seize the rebel priests they were looking for.

The military in power and the affluent minority—infamous alliance in fear—gave free rein to the CCC (*Comando de Caza de Comunistas*—Band to Hunt Communists), an instrument of the ultra-right organization called *Tradición, Familia, y Propiedad* sponsored by the political regime. The philosopher Tristán de Athayde, founder in 1934 of the Brazilian Catholic Action, said that the movement "is a reactionary group supported by the government and by financial interests."

The target of the CCC was the progressive clergy, then, of course, the "Red Bishop," and Bishop Brandao Vilela. The dictatorship carried the repression to an extreme: detentions, military occupation of universities, deprivation of rights by decree of the Executive, assassinations, and deportations—the whole vicious range of violence and terror. Fathers Darío and Pedro were imprisoned in the capital of Pernambuco for distributing a pamphlet deploring the misery of the people. Two United States priests assigned to that same diocese in Recife were expelled from Brazil after being freed from prison. One of them, Peter Grams, explained on returning to his country that, "We said that there were hunger, sickness, and lack of education while enormous sums were being spent on the military establishment."

In June, 1969, in a suburb of Recife, the corpse of a priest was found hanging from a tree. His chest was riddled with bullets and his throat slit. The victim was Henrique Pereira Neto, professor of sociology and advisor of Catholic youth in the diocese of Olinda and Recife. Why was he assassinated? Because he was auxiliary to Bishop Helder Cámara? He was first on a list of thirty-two condemned to death by the *Comando de Caza de Comunistas.* Obviously the "Red Bishop" was among the number.

The military dictatorship, pleased with the help the CCC gave it, took no action. The rich minority smiled arrogantly while the communications media which it controlled revealed their complicity by dead silence.

Father Lage Pessoa, a member of the Brazilian "Abrahamite" minority, expelled from the country by the official repression, described from his exile the political and social scene in his country.

A perfect mechanism of publicity, extensive and subtle, is permanently manipulated to persuade us all, including the dispossessed, that capitalism is freedom. Freedom of thought, freedom of expression, freedom of the press, freedom of worship, and who knows what other freedoms in contrast to a regime that all should suppress—nefarious Communism. Exceedingly contradictory theories thus spring up, such as the *Johnson Doctrine,* the counterpart of which in our countries is the *doctrine of ideological frontiers,* which make possible military dictatorships that negate all freedoms—justly, of course, in order to save them; assassinations and repressions in the name of freedom of opinion; book-burning and invasion of universities in the name of freedom of expression; persecution of bishops, priests, and Christian leaders in the name of freedom of religion.

Three Roads for Camilo

Various roads offering stimulating possibilities were open to young Camilo Torres Restrepo. Within his reach were the highest civil and ecclesiastical honors in areas compatible with his inclination for social work. He could have achieved the prestige and enjoyed the adulation which the traditional Colombian ruling class was accustomed to grant. His family, his cultivated mind, his handsome and impressive presence, and the influence itself of the profession he had chosen could provide him with all the requisites that the coalition of leaders of the establishment demand as prior conditions of those who wish high position and who would, then, acquiesce in the system of privilege. Colombia's ecclesiastical history provided him with three roads he might take: the one followed by St. Peter Claver; the one taken by St. Luis Beltrán; or the one chosen by Archbishop Antonio Caballero y Góngora.

Camilo Torres knew well the life story of the Jesuit Peter Claver, born in Catalonia in the midst of the misery prevalent among the workers of Urgel, who had come to Cartegena in the Indies to alleviate the misery there, unaware of the fact that the misfortunes of his childhood had been a fiesta compared to the situation that would meet his eyes in the New World. The black apostle, Alonso Sandoval, had shocked the Spain of his time by his denunciation of *pingüe,* the callous traffic in human beings.

Claver made Sandoval his exemplar in his efforts to alleviate the miserable sufferings of the blacks who, along with the putrifying bodies of the dead, arrived chained in the holds of vessels from Senegal, Guinea, Zambia, and Sierra Leone. In the bilge, which was pervaded by the stench of decayed flesh of those who had died during the voyage, Claver treated fevers and wounds of Mandingas, Felups, and Biafrans while high Spanish society diverted itself in the port city and filled the churches. To Camilo Torres that sainted slave of the blacks could be an example of service through sacrifice in direct, personal charity. Piety could provide the way. Camilo Torres saw that in the slums of Chambacú the situation of the blacks in Cartajena had not changed much in the three hundred years since their adored and patient champion, the Jesuit Claver, had passed among them.

Camilo also studied the brief history of St. Luis Beltrán who had confronted the *encomenderos* of the Caribbean coast. The favorite disciple of his Dominican brother, Las Casas, he was implacable toward the enriched oppressors whose misdeeds he denounced like a biblical prophet, yet was mild and understanding with the Indians. Legends circulate even today about this energetic missionary. The distress he caused *encomenderos* and colonial officials brought about his promotion to the position of Prior of Santa Fe de Bogotá. The tortures of conscience he suffered as he traveled the *altiplano* resulted in his return to Spain. Fray Bartolomé de las Casas had written him from Chiapas, Mexico, to "take special notice how you confess and absolve the conquerors and *encomenderos*." Beltrán's lack of decision, his courage, and his rejection by the oppressors who had placed him in high office ended his mission, and he died in Valencia in the odor of sanctity. Camilo Torres could, then, choose the exalted renunciation of the humble Dominican.

Another way, a triumphant one, was open to Camilo Torres. In 1781 when the *comuneros* of Socorro and Charalá brought over to their side the exploited peasants of eastern New Granada and marched in armed multitudes through the viceregal capital, Archbishop Caballero y Góngora, invested with full power, went out to meet them at Zipaquirá. In the town church he signed with the leaders of the popular movement some capitulations which recognized all the rights claimed by the insurrectionary peasants. Then, with a full *Te deum* he took an oath on the *Gospel* for the fulfillment of the provisions. The sworn word and the authority of the Archbishop appeased the *comuneros,* and the multitudes dispersed quietly and with confidence.

Quickly recovering their courage, the threatened families let loose a wave of repression against the humble. Leaders of the movement were beheaded and their heads exposed. Genocide prevailed in the villages where the uprising against the *alcabala* (transaction tax) and odious discrimination had begun. In recognition for his services, His Eminence, Don Antonio Caballero y Góngora became governor of New Granada. History recorded and glorified him as the "Archbishop Viceroy," an example for succeeding generations. Camilo Torres was free to choose the route that would make him vulnerable to the severe judgment of history by his country's writers.

He might have taken any of the three roads. Instead, he chose his own, the only one left open to him when he refused to submit to the authorities. It was the route laid out in accordance with what he saw within the protective citadel of medieval imitations, the ancient aberrations of Colombian society. He chose the road of armed struggle. Righteous anger blinded him as much to Heaven as to Hell. If the word of theologians that the ways of the Lord are inscrutable is accepted, it must be agreed that by his action Camilo Torres became a symbol for Catholic youth struggling against the tyranny of colonial institutions, both human and spiritual. With legitimate confidence, communists had been holding up the image of Ernesto "Che" Guevara de la Serna. Catholics could now acclaim with well-founded pride the image of Father Camilo Torres Restrepo. Poverty-stricken masses of the Third World and students demonstrating against an unjust social and political order, animated by the same just, youthful impulse, elevated the two images together.

Father Camilo's unsuspicious apostolic conscience and academic candor were shattered against an impenetrable wall. Everyone rebuffed him. His rejection may be explained on the basis of the fact that 2 per cent of his compatriots enjoyed on an average an income of 10,000 pesos a month per family; 80 per cent were in misery with a family income of 290 pesos a month, hardly enough for the barest necessities; the remaining 18 per cent, the middle class, had family incomes ranging from 890 to 3,200 pesos a month. Camilo Torres sought to arouse from their apathy the mass of peasants and urban laborers making up the 80 per cent of the population. But the great majority of them were debased by malnutrition, ignorance, illness, unemployment, and alcoholism maliciously cultivated by the State which makes production of liquor of the worst quality a fiscal means for keeping the masses in servitude and abjection. The middle class remained indifferent to the innovative enterprises of the rebellious clergy and were inclined to accept as true—as evidence of refined insight—the calumnies that spokesmen for the enviable privileged class poured out on them. Secondary funcionaries, small scale bosses, merchants, unemployed politicians, and professionals sought only to obtain favors from the establishment. The two per cent that enjoyed total power through the crushing force of their economic advantage and armed terror decreed a siege of the "evil one" who was trying to arouse the dispossessed.

The priest appealed to the most dependable for a unification of progressive movements made deaf by the rancorous stubbornness of their internal discord. Others were unscrupulous and ready to enter the coach of deceit at the sign of the first artful trick. The establishment hung on him the fashionable *sambiento* —they painted him red. Camilo Torres resisted, pointing out that, "Anti-communism has been more than anything a demagogic arm of the oligarchy."

Cardinal Luis Concha Córdoba, highest member of the Colombian Church, acting as grand inquisitor, applied to Camilo Torres the procedures of the Holy Office. He disregarded the doctrinal limits which the accused had made publicly: "The communists know very well that I will not join their ranks, that I am not now and never will be a communist, not as a Colombian, nor as a sociologist, nor as a Christian, nor as a priest." The condemnation which Cardinal Concha Córdoba handed down was no less severe than the one Bishop Manuel Abad y Queípo issued on October 16, 1810, against the priest Miguel Hidalgo: "Not only is the said project a sacrilege, but it is manifestly and notoriously heretical." They were giving him less and less room for action.

Camilo Torres, Chaplain of the University, sought support

among the students who acclaimed and followed him in the cities without serious risk. They thought it was one more local political circus like so many they had seen and applauded. Whey they finally understood, they fell silent and left him alone.

He was forced to resume the status of a layman. In the relentless persecution he suffered, the only choices open to him were defection or flight to the back country. He fled to the *selva,* convinced and desperate, mystical, practically alone. With tender simplicity he explained that he had taken that course because

As a Colombian, I cannot be foreign to the struggles of my people; as a sociologist, I have become convinced, thanks to the scientific knowledge I have of reality, that technical and efficient solutions will not occur without a revolution; as a Christian, I know that the essence of Christianity is love of one's fellow-man, and that only by revolution can we achieve the well-being of the majority; as a priest, I recognize surrender to our fellow man which the revolution demands is a *requisite of fraternal charity,* indispensable for the realization of the sacrifice of the Mass, not an individual offering, but one of all God's people through the intermediation of Christ.

Camilo disregarded the teachings of celebrated Catholic theologians. Of the four conditions for a just insurrection decreed by moral tradition—a just cause, a well-founded hope of success, ineffectiveness of pacific means, and decency in the means to be used—no more than two prevailed in Colombia at that time. There was no hope of success nor had pacific means been exhausted.

On February 15, 1966, an army patrol assassinated Father Camilo Torres and hid his body in the *selva.* The public notice which a government official transmitted to the priest's brother, stated, "The exact site of the burial is known only to the army."

Spokesmen for the establishment editorialized in their best style. "If Torres had been violent and foul-mouthed when he wore clerical garments, he was much worse when he assumed a peasant's garb." *(El Tiempo);* "The course of events has demonstrated that he was not such a progressive priest nor a modern type nor one of special sensibility." *(El Espectador).*

Silence in the Vatican. Paul VI, however, made Luis Concha Córdoba a cardinal for his wonderful guidance of the Colombian Church.

The Revolution of the Cassocks

Until December, 1968, the interests that dominated and manipulated ideas and honors functioned in peace. In that month the post-conciliar Church expressed itself anew from Buenaventura, a port on the neglected western coast of Colombia. The Bishop of that diocese, Gerardo Valencia Cano, along with forty-nine priests, signed a document which criticized the existing organization of Colombia, indicating that it was dominated by privileged castes, and proclaimed the necessity for revolutionary action against imperialism and the neo-classical bourgeoisie.

The Old Church, bulwark of the status quo, responded immediately: "It is inconceivable for some pastors of the Church to incite the people to revolution when their mission actually is to preach peace." It resorted to the usual hackneyed procedure, this time depersonalized and skillfully amplified by great fear. The Archbishop of Bogotá himself, Aníbal Muñoz Duque, declared the communists had infiltrated the Colombian clergy. The Bishop of Buenaventura was called with slight originality, the "Red Bishop." He was subjected to even more vituperation when he denounced the sale of the Vaupés Indians of the Amazon region as slaves with no one doing anything to stop the practice or provide a remedy.

The post-conciliar spirit began to rise again. Its previous irritating manifestation had coincided with Pope Paul's visit in Bogotá. Thirty young priests led by Father René García, parish priest of a populous slum, published a document in which they asserted that "inequality in Latin America will not be resolved through a choice between faith and life. A solution does, however, exist on the scientific level—revolution."

What the newspapers called "The Revolution of the Cassocks" quickly gained strength. Young, cultivated priests, trained in Belgian and French universities and accustomed to keeping up with European thought headed and enlarged the movement. They had served in Asia and Africa where they had intensified their pastoral vocation, and had returned from those regions with a greater interest in social change than in direct, out-dated proselytism.

The progressive clergy faced up to the ambiguity in the situation and to the encircling irrationality forged by those accustomed to justifying that irrationality promptly with the sort of propositions that they knew how to present as the repository of civilization and spiritual values. They were the local masters, also, of western culture.

Father Manuel Alzate Restrepo, priest in a parish of workers and unemployed blacks in Cali, who had been a post-graduate student in Strasburg and Lille and had been ordained in Paris, was accused by high members of the pre-conciliar hierarchy of Marxist tendencies because of the frank and happy nature of his initial work among his unfortunate parishioners. Earlier he had published a brief, succinct essay entitled "Conciliar Platform" in which, just before the meeting of the Eucharist Congress in Bogotá which Paul VI inaugurated, he presented to the world the true visage of the Colombian Church for which he held the priests responsible. Even though Rome as a part of the *aggiornamento* had suppressed the Index of Prohibited Books, the Bishop of Cali ordered the withdrawal and burning of Father Alzate's essay because he conceived it a "pamphlet born in a confused mind, a destructive blow against the Church of yesterday, today, and tomorrow." He would not listen to what the author had to say nor allow him an opportunity to defend himself.

When they learned that the Bishop had relieved Father Alzate of his parochial functions, the people pitched tents around the church and kept a continuous vigil to prevent the priest's forced eviction. The Archbishop of Cali, one of the pre-conciliar clergy, responded by excommunicating more than one hundred of the faithful who had supported Father Alzate. Twenty young priests of the Caucana Valley diocese also stood by him.

In view of the customary violence of the untouchables magnified by the hierarchy and then by the urban moderates, Father

Alzate pressed his complaints. In Bogotá, Cali, and Medellín progressive priests known as the Golconda group continued their denunciation of the conditions producing the destitution suffered by millions of their compatriots. In October, 1969, in Cali, Father Alzate and the priests Vicente Mejía, René García, and Manuel Currea were imprisoned for attempting to lead a demonstration in a symbolic effort to take over the University of Antioquia. The government and the Old Church accused them of defying the law and inciting a riot.

On October 21 the police broke into the parish church, San Juan Evangelista, which Father Alzate had served in Cali. Using tear gas they again dispersed the crowd which tried to prevent Father Luis Vallecilla, sent to replace Father Alzate, from assuming the charge. The pre-conciliar clergy promptly justified the State's repressive action. On November 1, 1969 the Archbishop of Cali, Alberto Uribe Urdaneta, wrote a long letter to the clergy of his diocese in which he characterized the rebel clergy "as agents following well-known Marxist tactics for destroying the Church."

Blinded by rancor and pride, Uribe Urdaneta let loose his herd against Father Alzate. When those carrying out the Archbishop's orders arrived at the Church of San Juan Evangelista and challenged the people, accusing their destitute and imprisoned former priest of "sacrilege" and "evil-doing," the crowd's anger became so intense that it could be quelled only by the police always at the service of the fashionable Archbishop, archetype of those indifferent to the post-conciliar spirit. He seemed to be that other pre-conciliar Church, doctrinally and temperamentally alien to the sufferings and the patience of the people. Anyone who, satanically, rejects the inevitability of misery—vouched for by averages, hypocrites, prohibitions, wheedlers, rules, subchanters, and organized powers—is, in the eyes of the Old Church, communistic, and must at least be put in jail in order to be free.

In Bogotá, Holy Week of 1969 culminated in a protest Mass celebrated by various young priests in a working class neighborhood. At the same time in Medellín, Colombia's second and most traditional city, Bishop Tulio Bolero removed two priests for having delivered "revolutionary sermons."

Among the people of Don Matías in a mountainous region of the Department of Antioquia, Abelardo Arias Arbeláez, the parish priest, brought down the archepiscopal wrath upon himself by instigating a revolution. Well prepared and an accomplished linguist, Father Abelardo had been ordained in Rome and had studied the situation of the poor in Asia and Africa. In his parish he founded a cooperative for keeping savings accounts, making loans, and granting credit at one per cent a month. The poor of Don Matías had paid ten per cent a month to obtain credit from the rich. On the grounds that handouts are humiliating, Father Abelardo organized a work program for the eighty-five destitute families in the parish, obtained houses for them at eighty pesos a month, and provided a cooperative service for obtaining food and medicine. After he purchased three trucks in the name of the parish to compete with the milk monopoly maintained by wealthy persons in the village, the producers obtained better prices, and milk was made available to the neighborhood poor.

In order that daughters of families with scanty resources might attend the parochial school directed by Capuchin nuns, he made arrangements to reduce the prohibitive requirement of four uniforms to one made of the least expensive material. When the nuns resisted, he accused them of giving their students a classical education with an aristocratic slant. He challenged them by proclaiming that, "In a Church built with the sweat of the peasants, I as parish priest cannot permit any girl to be rejected because she is poor."

From May 9, 1965, when Father Abelardo arrived in Don Matías, he was an object of suspicion to the rich people—he was a "red" priest. Unsuspecting and happy, Father Abelardo had stepped down from the bus that deposited him in the parish, his mind overflowing with exotic ideas and his body full of energy. In his luggage he carried the encyclicals of John XXIII and the conclusions of Vatican Council II, which he had read carefully, understood well, and joyously accepted.

He immediately incurred the ill will of the lords of the manor. Their dislike increased in proportion to the degree that the new priest carried forward his reforms, until Tulio Botero, Bishop of Medellín, heard of them. The Old Church united with the people of Don Matías who felt offended and hurt, and with the nuns who had left the parochial school. Father Abelardo received a definitive order: restore the situation to its former state. Father Abelardo, who had studied the works of Cardinal Leo Suenens of Belgium, replied, "The only man who blindly obeys the orders of his superiors is the soldier. There is considerable difference between a soldier and a priest."

In order that Father Abelardo should have no doubt about military discipline, soldiers were sent to Don Matías. Bolero sent the Vicar General to the village with a loud speaker which was installed on the balcony of the *alcaldía*. On market day, Father Abelardo could be accused before everybody; but the people booed the Vicar and laughed at him. Bishop Botero, even more irritated, named Father Santiago Echeverri curate of Don Matías. He arrived with a pistol in his belt and the backing of the police. The Old Church and the State were ranged against Father Abelardo, but his poor parishioners rallied to his support to protect him from the uniformed forces. With two pistols in his belt, Father Echeverri left the following week.

The Young Church in the Department of Antioquia became concerned. On September 21, 1969 newspapers in Medellín, the capital of the Department, published criticisms made by the city's clergy of the political-economic situation in Colombia. Father Guillermo Vega, Secretary of the Archdiocesan Synod, scheduled to meet there, called attention to the uneasiness of the post-conciliar Church. Father Vega's colleagues supported him unequivocally and directly. The Medellín presbytery declared, "There is actually a noteworthy marginal situation in this country. The people look upon our national leaders as strangers to their interests and demand a change in the government's attitude."

The Old Church, with Bishop Tulio Botero an arrogant example in Antioquia, was powerful in the Bogotá hierarchy and heir of Cardinal Concha Córdoba's pre-conciliar style. With its blessing, the government expelled from the country members of the religious order of Mary Mount from the United States who had been conducting a select school for young ladies. They were labeled

"Communists" because they required their students to take part in social service in a proletarian neighborhood of the capital city. Also several European priests, charged with "communist subversion," were expelled for having collaborated with the Young Church of Colombia.

Why do they not understand? The Minister of National Defense announced that the body of Father Camilo Torres Restrepo would soon be delivered to his family. Only the army knew where he was buried.

Two Hierarchies

Generals Juan Carlos Onganía and Augustín Lanusse attended short lecture courses on Christianity which the Old Church of Cardinal Antonio Caggiano had organized in La Montanera, a mansion in Pilar belonging to the Buenos Aires clergy. When the military regime, which had just deposed the constitutional government of President Arturo Illía, took possession of the ministeries, Cardinal Caggiano added to the pomp of the occasion with his presence.

However, the progressive clergy failed to endorse the questionable practices of the pre-conciliar Church, yoked to the cart of the victorious generals. The first evidence of their position came after the hierarchy failed by April, 1968, to alter its position toward the tyrannical economic and social situation. Twenty priests of Santa Fe, eight of Chaco, and seven of Corrientes condemned the regime.

The difficulties had commenced in one of the most populous neighborhoods of greater Buenos Aires. On September 25, 1964 John XXIII named Jerónimo Podestá Bishop of Avellaneda to serve that industrial suburb of Buenos Aires where about 300,000 workers were concentrated. He was so active in spreading among the workers and their families the views expressed in Pope John's encyclicals and in *Populorum Progressio* that he became known as "the Workers' Bishop." He was enormously popular in the slums. Nobody would have supposed that the Papal Nuncio in Argentina, Humberto Mozzoni, would pay any attention to the label *"peronis-*

*ta"*which businessmen and the government had attached to Podestá. In one of the darkest episodes in Argentinian ecclesiastical history, Mozzoni, compliant to the wishes of Gen. Onganía, persuaded Paul VI to remove Podestá from his position and, on December 4, 1967, name him Titular Bishop of Horrea Di Aninico. The forsaken Bishop lamented, "The disclosure of my renunciation and the motives which could be cited correspond to incentives I can manage to explain to myself and are ones which can damage me, but above all can damage God's people who are the Church."

The Papal Nuncio was to blame. An avalanche of protests from workers' organizations and from a provincial lay commission tried to penetrate the Vatican's shuttered windows. It was feared in Buenos Aires that Catholics would take over the Bishop's seat. Bishop Podestá's resignation prevented that; his successor in the diocese of Avellaneda, Antonio Quarracino, previously Bishop of Nueve de Julio, was a progressive. Podestá and Quarracino had inspired the "little Quilmes Council" which in June, 1965, with its pronouncements concerning priestly life, the position of the clergy in the Church, and their relation to the world, had begun to establish the bases of the Young Church in Argentina.

Elated by their triumphs the reactionary high clergy of Argentina sought to reach the widest possible audience. The archdiocese charged the priest Julio Meinville with the task of instructing the faithful. For his conferences in Buenos Aires and the provinces he found inspiration in a work called *Masonry within the Church* by a Frenchman, Pierre Virion. According to Meinville the spread of progressive ideas in Catholicism is a consequence of the influence of Jews, Masons, and Communists. He went about the country preaching the doctrines of the Old Church and denouncing the rebel priests. The pastoral mission committed to Father Meinville suffered from lack of listeners. It died one day without grief or glory.

The symptoms were ignored. Antonio Aguirre, Bishop of San Isidro, a diocese near Buenos Aires, deprived its parishes of five priests accused of being "worker-priests." That pre-conciliar Bishop affirmed, "The Church must not, itself, intervene in social problems." At the same time he authorized the government to expel four Spanish worker-priests from the country, accusing them of "preaching extremism and the resort to violence." They were Jesús Fernández Naves, Joaquín Fernández, Emilio Parajón, and the Jesuit Santiago Frank.

The two Churches were thus clearly defined. On May 1, 1968 four hundred members of the Argentinian clergy aligned themselves with the post-conciliar side, adding strength to the Priests' Movement for the Third World. In the same category were the twenty-one priests—worker-priests who labored in the factories—who, on December 20 of the same year, stood guard before the *Casa Rosada* [official residence of the President] to show opposition to the official plan for the ill-advised eradication of the *villa miserias.* The same post-conciliar spirit animated eleven Argentinian citizens and several hundred priests who four days later completed a fifty-hour fast in fulfillment of a Christmas Pledge to protest social injustices and the "sin of pride."

The Old Church would not permit it. The ancient Archbishop of Buenos Aires, Primate of Argentina, Cardinal Antonio Caggiano, declared, to the eternal gratitude of the military regime, that "the danger is that technical assistance offering guidance to the workers in temporal problems which is the function of union leaders will be substituted for religious assistance proper to priests." The young post-conciliar clergy disregarded such instructions. In March, 1968 at Villa Quinteros in Tucumán, they joined Father Fernández Urbana, to lead the proletariat who faced tear gas and the bullets of the police to ask for the reopening of the San Ramón sugar mill, closed a year and a half before with wages due its eight hundred employees nine months in arrears. The post-conciliar clergy of Tucumán had its baptism of fire in that struggle.

On January 1, 1968 the clergy gave support to the cause of the unemployed in the province. They promoted a labor day celebration in a province which had the highest index of unemployment and malnutrition in Argentina and the least consumption of milk—in a country which has 30,602,000 hectares of arable land, the largest agricultural area in Latin America. The police struck brutally. San José Obrero, a locally venerated saint, met the worst fate when the police cut his effigy to pieces.

In Tucumán thirteen minor clergy opposed the order from the capital city denying freedom of expression. Proudly they stated, "The protest of so many brothers cries out for justice, solidarity, witness, and compromise. This means making their problems and their struggles ours and being able to speak for them." Three priests, the Dominican Juan Ferrante, José García Bustos, and another disciple of the Belgian Cardinal Suenens, Armando Dip, who had proclaimed, "we are not the Bishop's employees," were the principal promoters of the movement which adopted as its motto, "Cry aloud, spare not" from the biblical text. [Isa. 58:1. King James Version.]

At the same time a group of thirty-eight priests in Rosario met to express their concern about Bishop Guillermo Bollati's lack of interest in social problems. They accused him of failing to communicate with the priesthood and of systematic obstruction of social action which Vatican Council II had inspired. They sent their complaints to the Congregation of Bishops at the Vatican. By April, 1969 as many as two hundred seventy Argentinian priests, including parish priests, members of church tribunals, administrators of ecclesiastical estates, and coadjutors, rectors, and professors of parochial seminaries and chaplains of Buenos Aires, Santa Fe, Entre Ríos, Córdoba, Tucumán, Chaco, and La Rioja, had accused their higher clergy of insensibility and threatened to resign. They asked the Holy See for canonical judgment. Bolatti went to Rome. Instead of considering his resignation from the bishopric of Rosario, Paul VI told him to arrange a dialogue with the rebellious priests.

Bolatti bore down heavily. He dismissed from the parish of San Pedro Apóstel in Cañada de Gómez Father Armando Amirati, one of the spokesmen of rebellion in the diocese who was loyally supported by the parishioners he had served for seven years. A Capuchin, Román María de Montevideo, was sent to replace him with the support of the police. The police opened fire, and several young people of the small Santa Fe town fell wounded. Later, a general strike in defense of Father Amirati paralyzed the town's operations. Bolatti sent out a victory party from Rosario which reported on the number of parishioners conquered for the Old Church. In Cañada de Gómez, however, he was obliged to sub-

stitute one of his diocesan auxiliaries, Monsignor Benito Rodríguez, for Father Ramón. The people stood by the post-conciliar
priest and took over the parish houses of the towns of Coronel
Bogado and Soldini.

Humberto Mozzoni returned in the middle of the affair. At
the Holy See he had been the one who had succeeded in getting
Jerónimo Podestá removed from the bishopric of Avellaneda. His
cleverness in bringing the rebellious clergy into line by use of
the military was rewarded a few months later by his transfer to
the Papal Nunciature in Brazil. He had blocked the dialogue
which Paul VI had counseled. The co-responsibility of the Church
in these times would extend beyond Italy. Its collective renewal
encountered an implacable antagonist in the pontifical representa-
tive. If he could prevent it, neither the laity nor the priesthood
would be allowed to participate in the progress of the Church.
The Church must continue being a medieval monarchy never
becoming a democracy. Mozzoni maintained an inflexible position.
He stated:

Ubi Episcopus, ubi Ecclesia. Only with a bishop does a Church
exist; without him, there is no Church. A bishop may have faults;
we may be more intelligent or cultivated than he is; but he is the
source of sacramental grace, the liturgy, the Sacrifice of the Mass.
He is the custodian, the depository, the authorized interpreter of
Divine Revelation, the official announcer of the Gospel. He who
breaks communion with the bishop, who fails to do him homage which
is homage to Faith and Charity, becomes a stranger to the Church,
attacking the unity of the religious community.

No one had defied Bolatti's authority in Rosario. He had simply
been asked to open the diocese to the instructions of the encyclicals and Vatican Council II. He had replied with ecclesiastical
censures and refusal to discuss matters. Resignations by priests
of the Young Church began to occur. The rebel priests, whose
agents were Fathers Armando Amirati, Oscar Lupori, Ernesto
Sonnet, and Francisco Parenti, insisted on their points of view.
In their opinion Bishop Bolatti had refused to direct his diocese
in accordance with conciliar orientations; he had failed to renew
the contract of the Spanish priests because of their "excessive

progressivism;" he had exceeded the limits of his authority in the centure *a divinis* of Pareti and José María Ferrari.

The Old Church, with Cardinal Caggiano and Nuncio Mozzoni, continued to be isolated, constantly more involved with the repression practiced by the dictatorship. General Juan Carlos Onganía from the *Casa Rosada* and Gen. Augustín Lanusse, military strongman of a powerful family of landowners, industrialists, and financiers, with a passion unusual in Argentina, took charge of suppressing the explosive popular discontent. Bishops Primatesta and Italo di Stéfano y Devoto, each in his own way, had censured the excessive repressions of the regime.

A considerable part of the Young Church had committed itself to the firing lines, with the post-conciliar priesthood at the forefront of the protest. In Colonia Caroya near Córdoba they met to take part in the Priests' Movement for the Third World led by Father Miguel Ramondetti. There, in the name of four hundred Argentinian clergy, efforts to "change the oppressors" and the possibilities of "no active violence" were laid aside, and the feasibility of armed struggle and the establishment of authentic socialism were examined. The group demanded the freeing of political prisoners. Immediately the hierarchy replied from Buenos Aires, to the gratification of the regime, "It would be naturalistic and anti-religious to subordinate the Church to the revolutionary process."

The military regime raised almost to a state of frenzy the brutal repression of economic, social and political non-conformity of the people whose demands the post-conciliar clergy supported. At that moment the Old Church reaffirmed its position from the Cardinal's palace with the statement that "the Church as well as the State is a perfect and necessary society with purposes and functions clearly distinguished. The Church has always collaborated with the authorities for the common good."

On the Other Bank of the River

The rebellion of the Argentinian priests crossed the Río Plata.

The golden legend of the "Latin American Switzerland" had vanished in the face of scarcities and fusillades, inflation, and terrorism. The post-conciliar Church aroused the priests of Villa del Cerro, an area of Montevideo striken in June, 1969 by a conflict between slaughterhouse workers and the government. The young Uruguayan clergy made common cause with the workers and aided those affected by the conflict. Some provided food for the strikers' families while others took part in street demonstrations and in dissemination of the laborers' demands, which they considered just.

The police searched for Father Juan Carlos Zaffaroni who had been accused of rebellion against the State. In Zaffaroni's opinion the possibilities were poor for a direct, armed confrontation with archaic yet vigorous structures. On national television he said that "armed conflict in Uruguay is a certainty," and that "the masses and leaders are ready for it as a consequence of their lack of confidence in the democratic regime."

Salto authorities urged the Bishop and priests of the diocese to condemn Zaffaroni and to give their blessings to the persecution directed at him as the Colombian hierarchy had done in the case of Camilo Torres. The hierarchy and priests of Salto limited themselves to declaring that "the motives which personally actuated Father Zaffaroni were within his pastoral choice." They added, in accord with the post-conciliar spirit, "His action in giving sacrificially his person and his life to the service of others gives us an example of Christian charity. Fraternally, we deplore that the dialogue, an indispensable condition for carrying out experiments of this sort, has not been maintained with the wisdom and to the extent necessary."

Between Lautauro and Maritain

The occupation of the Santiago Cathedral by members of the Camilo Torres Group was like an alarm bell arousing the young clergy and the parishioners of the Chilean Church. Those who occupied the Cathedral believed that Paul VI's journey to Colombia would be "the ratification of the alliance between the Church's hierarchy and the military and economic powers who were at the service of Yankee imperialism."

During the hours that the occupation lasted, three priests— Paulino García, a Spanish worker-priest ordered by the police to leave the country within twenty-four hours, Diego Palma, and Francisco Guzmán—had celebrated Masses within the Cathedral precincts, praying for the dead in Vietnam, for the Biafrans, for political prisoners in Brazil, and for all those in Latin America who are exploited. Among the laymen was the veteran Catholic union leader, Clotario Blest, who, from the Cathedral, recommended that Marxists and Christians draw together and accord homage to Commander Ernesto "Che" Guevara.

Cardinal Raúl Silva Henríquez, the most progressive among those of his rank in Latin America, attempted to persuade by lamentation. He decently wrapped his surprise in the tunic of patriotism, saying that, "The action of a few uncontrolled priests, in forgetting their mission of peace and love, has led a group of young people and laymen to carry out one of the saddest acts in the ecclesiastical history of Chile." The following day the Cardinal revoked the censure issued against the nine priests who had directed the occupation of the Cathedral. From the Vatican the distant *Osservatore Romano* ventured to pass judgment on those Chilean priests and the three nuns who accompanied them as persons "intoxicated with sociological visions."

"Sociological visions," said the Roman Curia, with the intent of centuring the energetic way in which the Chilean Church met social problems of the nation which had found in Cardinal Silva Henríquez a dynamic post-conciliar promoter. The Santiago episcopate provided an office for sociological investigation which mobilized a team of experts for scientific evaluation of the whole country, and undertook studies to understand and modify the evident popular indifference toward the tasks and mission of priests. The results of the research, which the Jesuit Renato Poblete submitted to a publisher in 1962, were valid. He recognized the urgency of doing away with the "priest-king," shaman of the pious and the ignorant in every social rank. For Poblete, as well as for his companion Father Alliende, "the Catholic Church is by nature in motion, not because it is decreed, but because it is activated toward a better comprehension of man."

Chilean bishops used such studies as a basis for recommending to Catholics that, rather than torturing themselves with penances, they dedicate themselves to self-education and personal discipline which would make them competent to serve "in a tenacious manner, constant and effective, as Christ serves you." The Chilean hierarchy used Lautaro, a national hero, as an example of the highest form of the "Christ-like." To make their point, they cited the communist poet, Pablo Neruda. According to the hierarchy, Lautaro encompasses the whole; imitating him suffices:

> He heeded the hurricane wind,
> He fought till his blood drained away,
> Only then was he worthy of his people.

The Chilean Church did not sleep. Two days after the occupation of the Santiago Cathedral three Spanish priests, two from Holland, and eighteen Chilean priests of the Valparaíso diocese renounced their pastoral charges—a total of twenty-three in a Church which has always deplored the scarcity of clergy. They took sides with their colleagues in Santiago and declared that "slowly we have been discovering that our Bishop has a different way of discharging service to God's people. Our loyalty requires us to renounce our charges." They asked for a renewal of the Valparaíso Church in accordance with the postulates of Vatican Council II. The Bishop of the port city, Emilio Tagle Covarrubias, proceeded with unaccustomed celerity to convoke an assembly of two hundred priests to deal with the matter. The anachronistic monarchical concept has not been practiced within the Chilean Church; it has worked as a team. May it be, henceforth, an awakened Church.

It would not take a very discerning person from Northern Europe to ascertain the antecedents of that tendency. Months before Chile's own ecclesiastical dignitaries had called attention to their situation by examining their errors and mistakes. Others continued to trust in the conclusions of a pastoral synod of priests, nuns, laymen, industrialists and workers, landowners and peasants, intellectuals and students which achieved the most self-critical examination of conscience of any Latin American community. It rejected the Church's tie with the privileged classes, repudiated the fatuity prevalent in the churches, and censured the Church's interference in the national system of education. A full internal confrontation in their bishops' orientations and instructions resulted which the Young Church hoped to see launched more aggressively. In daily contact with marginal groups, the awakened Church clarified its post-conciliar anxieties regarding its dignitaries. The parish base provided them with plenty of reasons.

By promising to rectify his pastoral policy, Bishop Tagle Covarrubias succeeded in getting the twenty-three priests who had resigned in the Valparaíso diocese to withdraw their resignations.

The Chilean Church has been the most advanced in South America. Catholic intellectuals began to read Jacques and Raissa Maritain thirty years ago. A new vision of Catholicism led them to disagree with the way the Church in their country, influenced and even manipulated by traditionalist, conservative priests, dealt with social and economic problems. Catholic intellectuals assumed new attitudes which obliged the Chilean Church to change its outlook and methods, while the rest of the Latin American hierarchy and priesthood were governed by the sectarian habits of the Spanish Church which was triumphant in its support of Francisco Franco and his military followers. The best pastoral anthology of that zeal may be found in the pastoral letters of the Colombian Miguel Ángel Builes, Bishop of Santa Rosa de Osos. Archeologists may find in them the folkloric excrescences of that sectarianism from which the Chilean Church had remained free.

As early as 1937 in Santiago the episcopate had issued a progressive pastoral letter concerning workers' wages. Twelve years later it published an instruction concerning the just use of material wealth. In 1962 two other documents—"The Church and the Problem of Rural Life," and "Current Social and Political Duty"—demonstrated a youthful aspect of the southern Church though it still exhibited certain traditional conservative values.

Hence no one could understand what happened to Father Vicente Alfieri through the action of Don Guardella, whose See was in Rome. Father Alfieri was distinguished for working among the parishioners of Renca in the outskirts of Santiago where his achievements had earned him the love of thousands of the downtrodden. One day an order came from Rome for his removal. The poor of Renca took possession of the church building "in order to pray for Father Vicente's return." No one listened to them.

The dispossessed classes were distressed by devaluations, inflation, demagogy, and scarcity. The social situation was raising problems of conscience among the priesthood so rapidly and so extensively that they claimed the attention of the hierarchy and even affected the Archbishop himself in 1969. The auxiliary Bishop of Santiago, Gabriel Larraín, resigned his position and left for Paris. The Cardinal explained the matter as "an honorable search for faith and direction, foreign to any morbid exhibitionism, and meriting the respect due one's own conscience." Two months later when Larraín's successor was consecrated in the parish of El Bosque, the Young Church interrupted the ceremony and read a resolution to protest the system of designating bishops, pointing out, however, that their action was not in disparagement of the prelate, Ismael Errázuriz. After a twenty-five-minute interruption the Cardinal succeeded in saying, "We are now and always have been disposed to listen to what the faithful of our Church wish to put before us. The Apostles Peter and Paul always consulted with the Church. The Church wants the most worthy to fill the position of bishop."

Cardinal Silva Henríquez was the only Latin American prelate to publicly denounce the assassination of Father Humberto Pereira Neto, aide to Bishop Helder Cámara in Recife, victim of the *Comandos de Caza de Comunistas* in Brazil.

By order of the Archbishop of Concepción, Manuel Sánchez, that same post-conciliar hierarchy turned over its property for construction of houses for poor families who began occupying them April, 1969. In his address at the opening, Bishop Sánchez explained that "God created the earth and all it contains for all men and nations; therefore the Church will re-examine its possessions in order to share them."

The Young Chilean Church is the most progressive in Latin America. In a country overwhelmed by the rapidly increasing scarcity of necessities which every day adds to the misery of the poor, an inevitable condition in all Latin American countries with no petroleum resources, no one dares label as communist those priests who make themselves worthy of their flocks. Such rationality must be attributed to Chile's high level of political culture to which communists have contributed for many years.

The Pond Becomes Turbulent

Paraguay is a country with a poorly fed rural population, free-running rivers, green meadowlands belonging to the few, and a personal military dictatorship which has held absolute power since 1954. Within an indifferent and overbearing Paraguayan autocracy, only the young clergy attempted to struggle for justice. Occasionally they were supported by medical students and others from the Catholic University who were customarily beaten up on the slightest pretext by the well-paid police of Asunción.

Illiteracy and anemia, a consequence of dependence on cassava root for food, are prevalent in this country where the farm workers do not own the land. Middle class professionals prefer to emigrate; so do the intellectuals. For example, Augusto Roa Bastos in Buenos Aires is dean of the exiles from a country half of whose people have abandoned their beautiful national territory. On top is the voracious group of landowners and smugglers protected by the army and pampered by the Pentagon.

For centuries the Church acquiesced to the powerful who were in control. In particular corners of the world opprobrium passes unnoticed. But some Paraguayan clergy had known the outside world. Others, as in the eighteenth century, had devoted their leisure to clandestine reading and prohibited news. Graham Greene, who visited the Guaraní nation in 1969, published in *Corriera della Sera* of Milan the most recent and impartial evidence available. After describing the infamous social panorama which has characterized General Alfredo Stroessner's military dictatorship, the English writer noted, "Only the Church (the Jesuits) seem to disturb the tranquil surface of that pool. A priest said, 'The new reality of the Church disturbs the President; he gets along well with the old monsignors; now he really does not know what is going on.' Stories about Camilo Torres, the priest killed by guerillas in Colombia who became the Catholic counterpart of Che Guevara, infiltrate the frontiers."

The breach between the Church and the dictatorship began the day the government expelled four members of the Society of Jesus from the country on grounds of subversion. After that the hierarchy took the part of the progressive Church and denounced "the flagrant violation of human rights" in Paraguay. The Church was trying to determine the proper limits of action, but the government would not cooperate: it kept in force a public act stating that the government and its party, the National Republican Association, "are Catholic, Apostolic, Roman." Stroessner refused a face-to-face meeting and set up a smoke screen with the statement that, "By a deliberate and conscious act of will, my government pledges itself to worship God, practice Christian principles, and protect the religion of the people."

This new Dr. José Gaspar de Francia was opposed at this juncture by Jesuit intellectual guerillas who entered the struggle suddenly and then lay in ambush. Taking advantage of a favorable occasion, they disappeared—the flea's tactic. The weekly organ of Paraguay's Episcopal Conference, *Comunidad,* risked saying openly a few days before his arrival in Asunción that Nelson Rockefeller, President Nixon's envoy, is the "leader of the liberal wing of the Republican Party and the only one who believes in it, and bears a name identified with the Standard Oil Company and has a strong odor of petroleum exploitation."

The post-conciliar Church went on record openly against the dictatorial regime during the last days of August, 1969. A message from the Paraguayan bishops to the National Congress expressed complete disagreement with a projected law which General Stroessner had sent to the legislative body. Cleverly devised to further his boss rule, the proposed law under the sham title, "Defense of Democracy and Political and Social Order of the

State," was intended as a more effective substitute for a repressive act which had been in force since 1953. It was necessary to adjust the judicial machinery of the tyranny to the exaggerated fear which pervaded it.

The bishops formulated juridical and philosophic criticisms of the autocracy's proposal. They expressed anguish and concern about its contents and called attention of the legislators to their responsibility in the procedure in carrying out the law. Their spirited message stated in part that "the projected law would consecrate a form of totalitarian absolutism condemned by the pontiffs. . . . Progress for Paraguayans requires profound changes in the economic-social order, with the inevitable risks which that implies and which must be assumed collectively with courage and without delay of any sort."

One should not back down before a perverse and flexible intelligence. In the preceding century Dr. Francia had acted accordingly and had governed for thirty-five years. It was intended that no one should fall into the bad habits of the rest of the world and, through them, be contaminated by what the progressive clergy of Latin America were thinking and doing, especially in countries having common boundaries with Paraguay—Brazil and Argentina. Fear built up the barriers of solitude. Censorship became proportionately more severe as the Young Church revealed its course. Very little information came out of that seclusion. What did become available indicated that the dictator's pedestal was crumbling and that domination by a small group of great landowners, potentates of corruption and slavery, was growing.

Stroessner was frightened and irritated on becoming aware that the Church was no longer pliant, somnolent, and in the dictator's pocket. The hierarchy had striven hard to find partial remedies. The situation became so tense that the sickly alarm of the empresarios of the legal order led them to view the apostolic persuasion as subversive. Persecution was suddenly let loose.

In Asunción the Catholic University students rallied to the support of their Jesuit teachers. In the first disputes with members of the University, the regime lost its head and on October

22, 1969 expelled from the country Francisco de Paula Oliva, Jesuit professor of philosophy. As a protest and means of vindicating themselves, priests, nuns, and students carried out at night a Way of the Cross around the university buildings. Using spiked clubs, the police interrupted the ceremony, wounding a number of participants, including the seventy-three-year-old Jesuit Juan José Gómez Rocafort. In accordance with Canon Law the Archbishop of Asunción, Aníbal Mena Porte, excommunicated those who gave the order and those who carried it out for "putting violent hands on the persons of the clergy or religious of either sex." Vatican radio in a French language broadcast on November 2, reported the incident as "brutal aggression" and honored Father Gómez Rocafort, saying that "For some time the rights of man have been better defended in Paraguay by students, Catholic or other, than by the government police of the General *Father of His Country.*"

The excommunication which Archbishop Mena Porte decreed included the Minister of the Interior, Sabino A. Montanaro, the Chief of Police of Asunción, Colonel Francisco A. Britez, and other functionaries of the dictatorship. Stroessner made himself a canonist in order to impugn the action. According to his interpretation, "The application of Canon Law certainly has validity when it testifies for the faith but not when it is in conflict with the law." He resorted to the argument invoked by other South American governments in ordering expulsion of priests of the Young Church. "Clerical garments are not a shield nor do they provide immunity, especially when three or four foreigners attempt to foment agitation in the country."

Then Stroessner dictated the law. He bleated that "The Paraguayan Government will not tolerate having those who oppose the laws take refuge in sacred orders in order to incite actions contrary to law." While the dean of South American dictators celebrated his fifty-first birthday among people humbly bowing, and while his exiled compatriots in Argentina made common cause on Buenos Aires avenues with the Young Church of their country, priests and nuns were recovering in clinics and oratorios from the floggings and oppression which had been their reward for endeavoring to lessen the miasma arising from the pool.

Religion, the Opiate of the People

The colonial heritage, congealed on the crest of the Andes, broke out like fireworks in guerilla activities and political eccentricities: General René Barrientos' acrobatics, General Ovando Candia's duodenal ulcer, and Regis Debray's pre-adolescent tropical odessy. Nothing, however, changed the oppressive misery of the miners. The icy winds of fright blew as always. Only the price of tin, which accounts for 80 percent of Bolivian exports, moved regularly downward. Revolutions come and go, and the Indians' condition has hardly changed from colonial times under the *encomenderos* to the present.

By 1967 a few Bolivian priests had begun to promote reform in their Church. In that year they initiated a movement to alleviate the suffering of Bolivian miners. Forty of them became involved with union demands in the mining districts and began to favor post-conciliar positions. They aroused the interest of the episcopate in working conditions in the mines, unchanged since the time when the Patiños and the Aramayos were the owners. They opposed some pastoral decisions, demanding the *aggiornamento* in their country's Church. On one occasion they placed themselves at the entrance to the mines but were forced to retire when the troops, in accordance with the law, threatened to drown the workers' protest in blood.

In the midst of a situation affected by the creaking camouflage of the Green Berets, by the fatuous flames of a disciplined left in the delegation, by the CIA seated at the official desks in La Paz, and by the daily occurrence of the unexpected, action by the Young Bolivian Church passed unnoticed on account of its timorous and provisional nature. Like other tools for subjugating and distracting the people, eighty-two per cent of the Bolivian clergy is imported.

The indigenous people dull their hunger by using the sacred

herb of the Incas. It provides them with energy for their forced labor in the highlands. According to Antonio de Ulloa, who discovered in the colonial period that the people chewed leaves of the coca plant, "The herb is so nutritious and invigorating that the Indians work all day without any other food, for it prevents them from becoming hungry."

If the politicians have made a daily carnival to divert them, then religion has been the drug which has kept the Indian bound in slavery. The majority of foreign priests reinforce the general tendency of the conformist Church to collaborate with the establishment, no matter how its outward appearance may vary, thus giving their support to political currents opposed to any profound change. The Cardinal is an Austrian, the Redemptorist Clemente Maurer. The Chaplain of the Army, Andrew Kennedy, is from the United States. The first was accused of having sold the manuscripts of Fray Bartolomé de las Casas which had been kept in the convent of San Felipe Neri. They are now the property of the Creole Petroleum Company of Caracas.

Neither Maurer nor Kennedy nor the rest of the eighty-two percent of the clergy who are foreign is concerned with the post-conciliar orientations which would benefit the indigenous masses. The national minority of the clergy, displaced and strangled, struggles between the hierarchy indifferent to the fate of the peasants and miners on the one hand, and the politicians who have sacrificed millions of lives as offerings to their own shamelessness on the other.

When Disillusionment Comes

In the lower Andes along the Pacific, the Peruvian Church could, if it chose, take pride in its courtly persistence in support of minority governments. With the Church's roots deep in the colonial epoch, history could serve as a key to explain the lack of genuine Catholicism among the Peruvian masses. It was a savory tradition which must have greatly influenced the spirit of the Archbishop of Lima, Cardinal Juan Landázuri Ricketts, in fixing the position of the Church with relation to the military government of his country. Was not the time ripe for modifying it with certain provisions?

Cardinal Landázuri Ricketts could not prevent the Church from being affected by the wave of nationalism which he realized was being stimulated to justify the *coup d'etat* against an unobjectionable, popularly elected government. The nationalization of United States petroleum installations generated great questions which choked off interest in other matters of importance. Henceforth, the Cardinal supported nationalization, and at the same time — waters sooner or later seek their level — prayed for a return "to the sane exercise of democratic suffrage and constitutional normality."

University students also understood the implications of the situation. They took to the streets to voice their protest against censorship of the press and persecution of independent journalists. When the police beat up students within the precincts of the Catholic University of Lima with the Rector, Father Felipe Macgregor, alongside them, they demanded that General Velasco Alvarado personally give them full satisfaction and security.

In the infuriating euphoria which the military in power created through conciliatory revisions, it was possible to assert that the Church, according to data provided by the Lima municipal tax list, was the largest proprietor of real property in the center of the capital. It was alleged that the Church owned some ninety blocks in the heart of Lima worth approximately twenty million dollars. The hierarchy made no denial. Four months later the Thirty-Sixth Episcopal Assembly approved the creation of a commission to assess socioeconomic matters and determine how the wealth of the Church could best be used.

Cardinal Landázuri seemed to be managing everything with discreet sagacity unknown to his predecessors in the Archbishopric of Lima when he got out of any difficulty in connection with the disappearance of his Bishop Coadjutor, Mario Renato Cornejo Ravadero (Cupid's pranks in the sacristy, it was found out finally in this sensational police case) and on the resignation from their charges by eight priests in the Trujillo diocese.

Some weeks before, Archbishop Carlos María Jurgens had angrily dismissed from their charges in Trujillo the Spaniards Mariano Cortés, Gonzalo Martín, and Carmelo Boni all of whom belonged to the wing of the Peruvian clergy most active among the workers. Their crime had been to head a quiet protest march against the opening of the luxurious quarters of the Trujillo Country Club, and at the same time to give support to a strike of workers whose wives had occupied the cathedral in the city. The Archbishop who had himself engaged the priests to take part in OCSHA *(Obra de Cooperación Sacerdotal Hispanoamericana* [Priestly Work of Hispanic American Cooperation]) now proposed to send them back to Madrid under a cloud. Jurgens, ostentatious exponent of the Old Church, immediately scorned the protest of the eight priests of his diocese who had resigned in sympathy with the priests who had been punished.

The following day Trujillo's pre-conciliar hierarchy dismissed seven more priests from their duties. Immediately new resignations brought the total to twenty-one. Churches were closed throughout the province and Sunday Masses suspended. Jurgens had to back down—he restored the three worker-priests of the original conflict. Restored through the backing of thousands of the faithful, and to the expressed satisfaction of Cardinal Juan Landázuri Ricketts, the priests promised to continue their "prophetic denunciation" which they had understood as an "obligation to call attention to any injustice on every occasion and in every circumstance." To give their rebellion wider appeal they stated that they shared "all the proposals of Camilo Torres who had the courage to denounce social injustices and to confirm his words with the sacrifice of his own life." They declared further that, "We do not necessarily believe that to achieve the objectives of the true Church we must become guerillas. Each situation in any given moment has its strategy. We do not repent the action we took against the Country Club, even less our having supported the workers in their just demands. We shall continue acting as we have in the conviction that we are on the right road."

The outcome of the conflict with Jurgens, which had occurred in the Department of La Libertad, encouraged priests in ONIS

(*Oficina Nacional de Intervención Social* [National Office of Social Assistance]) with offices in Lima, Arequipa, and Trujillo. In a document of nineteen chapters they analyzed the importance of agrarian reforms and made it a requirement of conscience binding for all Peruvians. When the military government hesitated, the post-conciliar priests justified confiscation of land by explaining and preaching that, "The ends of agrarian reform and the insupportable situation of secular injustice suffered by a majority of our nationals give ethical basis not only for the most radical forms of expropriation envisioned by actual legislation, but even the confiscation of wealth and rights to change in management of property which the aforesaid reform implies." The document was attached to the doctrinal directives of *Populorum Progressio,* while the politicians kept a sharp lookout for a chance to climb on Elijah's coach in which the Assumptionists always travel.

In Trujillo Archbishop Jurgens had to agree with the post-conciliar priests, but in Lima from the seat of government, the military refused to do so within the bounds which define revolutionary positions, leaving to the progressive clergy the doctrine and practice of complete reform in rural districts. Suspicion gathered that agrarian reform might have cooled the tentative revolutionary impulses of the new regime which was disposed to maintain the establishment in order to stay in power.

In order to work out for the time being difficulties in relations with the military who were in power, conclusions were set forth in the first-week pastoral letter of Arequipa (which, in October, 1969, thirty laymen and one hundred fifty priests and members of religious orders supported) announcing the necessity for separation of Church and State as the only means of loosening the restrictions which had reduced trust in the hierarchy of the Peruvian Church and had reduced its liberty and dignity since the time of the *benedícite* of Fray Vicente de Valverde in Cajamarca in the sixteenth century.

Between Two Terrors

Thistle or flower, the post-conciliar rebellion in Central America, especially in Guatemala, grew very slowly. Silently and sluggishly the Church began to come out of its compliant somnolence of centuries. In a country where a spade thrust in the earth would uncover a rifle, according to the graphic expression in an European magazine, terrorists of the right had made shooting a favorite type of outrage against the clergy. They sought to intimidate those who shared, though with diminished force on account of the fear which permeated the atmosphere, the modern ecclesiastical orientations. If in any part of the world the *aggiornamento* implied an absolute revolution, vertical and horizontal, it was in Central America. In the turbulence the Guatemalan Church had chosen to remain silent. Whom did that silence benefit?

Guatemala's rate of population growth, exceeding 3.4 percent a year, is one of the highest in the world. The illiteracy of the indigenous people who are the major element, is as much as 79.4 percent in urban centers and 92 percent in rural districts. The inflexibility of the Guatemalan social system and the explosive pressures it generates serve to explain the generally unsettled condition in Latin American countries.

The lines in Guatemala's hand did not foretell this depraved hemorrhage. It began under the military regime of Colonel Enrique Peralta Azurdia who took control of the State with the blessings of the landowners and the municipal manipulators. In vogue was the chimerical ideology that only the armed might of revolutionary groups could be counted on to overthrow the oppressive established order. Any ruffian or visionary fancied himself a Fidel Castro. Various leftist groups fortified themselves in the mountains. Guerilla action in Guatemala coincided with the increase in that same strategy of impatience in Venezuela, Colombia, and Peru. Havana granted the insurrectionaries more radio time than real help in men, arms, or supplies. Washington deployed against the rebels the perfected efficacy of the Green Berets, dexterous in the extermination of popular armed movements in forests and swamps. The Guatemalan guerillas were decimated by the Green Berets, a body created by the whimsical Pan American imagination of President John F. Kennedy as an auxiliary force to the Alliance for Progress and the Peace Corps and intended, under his orders, to provide for our protection.

With the unnecessary license of the government of President Julio César Méndez Montenegro and the enthusiastic support of the mercenary army, the CIA turned over to rightist organizations, entrusted with carrying out terror, the task of taking reprisals against the urban left. "The White Hand" became the most famous with its practice of seizing persons in their homes and assassinating them. They were taking revenge against the open violence of the extreme left in the mountains. The effectiveness of "The White Hand" prompted its sponsors to put it into operation later in Brazil under the name "Band to Hunt for Communists." In Guatemala between 1965 and 1968 there were three thousand victims of assassination as a result of the plan. Bishop Mario Casariego pled for cessation of the blood bath. Nobody listened to him.

Cautiously some elements of the progressive clergy began taking part in the struggle. Punishment was inflicted on three members of a religious order from the United States, Fathers Thomas and Arthur Melville and Sister Miriam Peters of the Maryknoll Order of Ossining, New York. In the course of their mission among the needy peasants of Huehuetenango they managed to come into contact with guerillas whom they provided with medicine and money. Prepared to teach children of the rich, they were unable to keep their distance from the poor; they were accused of organizing a guerilla movement known as the "Camilo Torres Front." In January, 1967 they were expelled from the country occupied by the Green Berets. Foreigners could not intervene in the internal affairs of the country; the government carried out the constitution. First, the two priests and the nun were declared common offenders, then the Old Church declared them apostate.

The fanatic persecution by "The White Hand" became so intense that on May 10, 1968 the bishops issued a pastoral letter deploring the rightist terrorism devastating the country. Bishop Casariego assumed a propitiatory attitude. He had alienated the great landowners by reiterated condemnation of the violence they had sponsored. They came to feel that the hierarchy threatened their systems of oppression to a greater degree than the guerillas who were disbanded in great disorder. In April, 1968 the coffee plantation owners ordered the abduction of Bishop Casariego. The anti-communist forces captured him on his return from a trip to Mexico. For three days they threatened him, demanding that he engage the Church in a move to the extreme right. When six auxiliary bishops declared that they would never lend themselves to political blackmail "if the abduction had such objectives," Casariego was freed in the vicinity of Quetzaltenango, refusing to say anything about his captors. What he would have to say would be whispered only at the Holy See behind closed doors.

Rome is shrewd. Casariego was called there after being freed. A year later Paul VI named that native of Spain the first Central American cardinal. Bells of the capital's eighty churches rang out in his honor. Tension was heightened between the poorly dissimulated annoyance of the aspirants to petty tyrannies and the frank, criminal hostility of the landowners who cultivated their coffee plantations with slave labor. Between the two terrors the Guatemalan Church, like the Venezuelan, preferred to keep silent.

Solentiname is an Archipelago

Suppressed, challenged, the post-conciliar winds gained strength little by little in the rarified atmosphere of Central America. Seculars and priests assembled in Nicaragua for two weeks at the beginning of 1969. They considered their past errors and projected their obligations in accordance with the orientations of Vatican Council II, the encyclicals of John XXIII, and *Populorum Progressio.* Three young priests—Ernesto Cardenal, a poet; Federico Argüello, a historian; and Enrique Mejía Vilchez, a theologian—urged the adoption of a post-conciliar line with the discreet encouragement of the Bishop of Chontales. At the close of the assembly the Jesuit León Pallais, Rector of the University of Central America, stated the opinion that its results indicated that, unfortunately, "Nicaragua suffers the disgrace of having a cowardly Church."

Cowardly? It would be more accurate to speak of a crushed

Church. As much as possible, the Bishops of Chontales and Matagalpa kept the Nicaraguan Church from languishing under the grimaces and ostentation of the despotism.

Since February 21, 1923, when Anastasio Somoza ambushed and defeated the guerilla, Augusto César Sandino, the victor set up a political and economic monopoly over the spoils. Nicaragua became the well-tended estate of one family. His position, made possible through the occupation of his country by the United States Marines, "Don Tacho" dedicated his life to the service of the United States in Nicaragua and the Caribbean with devoted abnegation until his death in 1956 in the Gorgas Hospital in the Panama Canal Zone. An unknown assailant shot him during a fiesta in León. In order to extract the bullet lodged near his spine, he had been transferred in a military plane which President Eisenhower personally ordered.

The Church, through the highest echelon of Managua's hierarchy, was a secular arm of "Don Tacho's" tyranny. It was as faithful as the National Guard which administered the subjugation and as friendly as Washington which was entrusted with the logistics of spreading fear. On the death of this accomplished practitioner of nepotism, his sons inherited his wealth and shamelessness. Their continued enjoyment of both was guaranteed by the triumvirate of Washington, the Old Church, and the National Guard which sustained Central American satrapies to the oppression of human rights.

The popular exasperation came to the surface one day in a protest against the farcical election of "Tachito" Somoza. The majority of the people tried to prevent him from becoming president of the republic. The climax occurred on January 22, 1969, on the Avenida Roosevelt in Managua when the National Guard discharged their machine guns at the crowd leaving a toll of more than forty dead and a hundred wounded. Leaders of the opposition took refuge in a hotel which the executioners surrounded. The ecclesiastical hierarchy with the Archbishop of Managua, Alejandro González y Robleto, at their head as always on similar occasions, sent a message supporting the government, and at the same time the Apostolic Nuncio, Sante Porta Lupe, and the military attaché of the United States urged the unconditional surrender of the members of the opposition who had sought refuge in the hotel.

In the assembly of 1969 the Young Church remained composed with a stern recommendation to the hierarchy and priesthood denouncing social injustices and urging that the Church "should not limit itself to evangelizing but should engage as well in advancing man toward his full liberty." The progressive Church sought rectification, through pressure exercised from below by social priests and the most outstanding of the faithful, of the Church's adhesion to the economic and political family dictatorship exercised for thirty-five years through police terror, pauperization of the people, and the shotgun imposition of a court of flashy dandies. Consequently an absence of ambiguity could be expected from the assembly of priests and laymen which met at the beginning of the year. It accused the Church of "collaborating conveniently with the government and forgetting the country's scars, misery, ignorance, and the existence of persecution."

Not only has the conformist Church collaborated with the tyranny for a long time, it has carried on a calculated, timid, and frivolous complicity with it. By radical contrast the Young Latin American Church found a wonderful model established in the archipelago in the Great Lake of Nicaragua known as Solentiname. The poet and philosopher, Ernesto Cardenal, had established a work center there which spread the new spirit of conciliation, equipped humble people to temper their subjugation while remaining believers, and restored dignity to the humiliated, liberating them from debasing charity.

The confrontation of the two Nicaraguan Churches will be a long-drawn-out affair. The young churchmen—the intellectual and popular Cardenal, Argüello, and Mejía Vilchez, among others —endeavored to restore confidence in the Church among peasants and urban groups and to reconcile them to their ministers. It seemed possible that the people might join them in a task which could end by disclosing the real Nicaragua to view; hardly an illusion, because its mask had been blessed by the Old Church in its work of excessively limiting any outreach.

Colonialism, Voodoo, and Communists

Of the viruses which underdevelopment promotes, militarism usually has greatest expansive force and is the most recalcitrant. It is cultivated in the test tubes of Washington for the solace of investors without imagination and for the entertainment of ingenuous university researchers. The coups against democratic regimes in Argentina and Peru in 1962 and in Guatemala and Ecuador in 1963 were followed in September of that year by the military coup against the popularly elected government of Juan Bosch in Santo Domingo. In that republic military juntas, the United States military occupation, and finally, Joaquín Balaguer's manipulations were all related to preventing Trujillo's disappearance from being detrimental to the economic systems established by his family dictatorship. The changes made were superficial and in accordance with the needs of the bourgeoisie who had flourished in the morasses of adulation they had accorded the despot. The economic and social base of the oppressive system was maintained, complete and powerful.

The Church had been one of the supporters of Trujillo's tyranny. It continued its role in the new order with abundant benefits however superficially they may be calculated. Forced indirectly by the plain clergy, who moved among the poor in crowded slums and knew and shared the privations of the rural population, the ecclesiastical authorities recognized the necessity of making known what property they possessed. After the Rockefeller cyclone had passed over Santo Domingo, an account of the damages it left revealed two dead, many wounded, and more than two hundred imprisoned. President Balaguer gave his explanation, a la Trujillo, to the pleasure of the producer of the spectacle, with the statement that "This is a continental communist conspiracy in which the priests of the revolutionary sector of the Church participated."

The Dominican Church, sullied by years of abjectness, sought to purify itself in the popular struggle. Labeling the priests of the Young Church communist impressed nobody, except the communists perhaps. In an interview, Faustino Fernández Ponto of *Excélsior,* Mexico City, asked Balaguer in Santo Domingo, "Why do the priests take part in agitation?" Behind his spectacles, Balaguer glanced to one side. He replied, "Because they want to better living conditions."

In that same violent Caribbean of the buccaneers, the high Puerto Rican hierarchy, without a single exception, is colonialist in point of view. Nothing prevents it from presenting itself in the characteristic pattern of the Old Church, conformist, totally integrated with the apparatus of the occupiers. The disfiguration of the island's culture has found the Church submissive. Its devotion has been reflected in the eagerness, the vehemence, and the rigor with which it has silenced the priests who have refused to participate in the distortion of the historical spirit of Puerto Rico or have endeavored to maintain its genuine cultural image. An example of that tendency of the Puerto Rican Church was the arbitrary sanctions taken against Father Ivan Illich which forced him to transfer his capabilities as a social investigator to Cuernavaca.

A few years later, in August, 1969 the four diocesan bishops of Puerto Rico, headed by Luis Aponte Martínez, after studying the matter for an hour prohibited the Spanish Jesuit Salvador Freixedo from celebrating Mass, hearing confessions, or exercising any other priestly function in the country. Why? Because in his book, *Mi Iglesia Duerme (My Church Sleeps),* Father Freixedo had passed judgment from within, as a "soldier of the ranks," on pastoral and liturgical deviations of the Old Church in America. The author began by stating his position precisely:

For centuries the Church advanced majestically along a broad road which slowly has become so narrow that it is no more than a dead-end alley. And certainly it is not easy to see its truth at first sight, especially by Christians who may not be accustomed to reflect on problems of life and faith, nor to interpret the unmistakable signs of the times. Nevertheless, this dead-end alley in which we find our Church is becoming for many Christians of the vanguard a matter of intense concern as they see Her, impelled by the inertia and blindness of many who lead Her (in spite of some voices among the hierarchy sounding the alarm), continuing to proceed without regarding the fact that there is no way out of the road they follow. The only way out is to stop at once and reverse directions. Except among a few, this is not being done.

The four bishops of the Old Church did not discuss the matter. They studied Father Freixedo's clear and courageous propositions for an hour. They chose the two expedients characteristic of the Old Church in similar cases: inquisitorial judgment of false contumacy for the author and the Index for the book. A group known as "The Awakened Church," in which some Jesuits took part, protested against the arbitrary decision of the colonialist Puerto Rican Church.

The Puerto Rican bishops had censured Father Freixedo in 1969 without giving him an opportunity to defend himself, when at the same time on another Antillean island heresies, liturgical monstrosities, and numberless pastoral aberrations were going unnoticed. The sound of Catholic bells in Haiti, morning and evening, in the countryside and cities beset with terror, mingled with the rhythm of drums sounding the measures of African ancestral ritual dances. The atmosphere harmonized their sounds and merged their evocations. The *hungan* and the *mambo,* with the paroxysms of fatigue from dancing all night by the *loa,* attended Mass and walked alongside the priest at the head of the procession. No one thought it wrong.

Pious images and the Cross itself had been converted into fetishes placed in shabby family sanctuaries. Walls of the *humfó* were adorned with chromos of saints who had become part of voodoo identified with mythological Africans; required Catholic holy days coincided with noisy voodoo celebrations. The synthesis has infinite expressions. The liturgy, prayers, holy water, and the Host all have recognized effectiveness in "putting the *loa* in motion." The Sorrowing Mother's image represents Ezili-fréda-Dahomey. Her jewels and her pierced heart evoke the riches and love of a voodoo divinity.

For five and a half million Haitians, half of whom are unemployed and 90 percent illiterate, who have a life expectancy of only forty years, and whose per capita income of seventy dollars a year is one of the lowest in the world, the voodoo, in the creole dialects, had always been a semi-official religion until François Duvalier came into power. His life-long tenure as president gave "Papa Doc" official status for practicing an arbitrary power without limits. Duvalier made use of the magic of voodoo as much as he did the fulminating cruelty of the *ton-ton macoutes,* his force for ceremonial encounters, and the ecclesiastical hierarchy, all of them mixed together. The Old Church in the shadow of the *mambo,* the *hungan,* and the *hûnsi* became a part of the Haitian tyranny. When the progressive clergy tried to rescue the dignity of their mission, henchmen burst into temples and seminaries. On August 16, 1969 the Department of Culture expelled a dozen post-conciliar priests from Haiti along with Doctor Pierre Cauvin, leader of one of the democratic front parties opposing the dictatorship which also included the Haitian Communist Party.

Two months later, on October 16, *Nouveau Monde,* "Papa Doc's" propaganda organ, announced that seven priests and two seculars had been expelled from the country accused of belonging to a leftist group, of attacking the Catholic hierarchy, and of planning a *coup d'etat* against the dictator. The Young Haitian Church had begun denouncing the religious deformations of voodoo which the "president for life" had maliciously condoned for the purpose of political domination and for furthering his pretentions of nationalizing the Catholic hierarchy in order to set up an autonomous clergy through the ignominious means of his dictatorship.

From Port au Prince under the direction of Archbishop Ligonde, the Old Church acted in collusion with Duvalier's intentions. Under public pressure the young professors at the Seminary and College of San Marcial were evicted from their classrooms with the acquiescence of Archbishop Ligonde. He took charge of the building and assigned another teaching group to the institution to replace the rebel priests whose prestige had grown in the intelligent discharge and post-conciliar spirit of their important cultural and religious duties.

The *ton-ton macoute* threw out of Haiti the priests Max Dominique, designated by the regime as leader of the Haitian Progress Party, Antoine Aderien, Rector of the Seminary of San Marcial, Ernest Verdieu, William Smarth and Paul Dejean, co-directors of the Youth Library, Pierre Yves Dejean and Joseph Hilarie along with civilians Joseph Romey and Niclero Casian. All this was happening while the arrogant potentates of Latin America, terrified, put pressure on their lock-step governments to maintain a *cordon sanitaire* around Cuba to protect their tribute system of anti-Christian profit from the surplus produced by the oppressed.

The Cuban Church condemned the blockade of the island and requested its termination. In his pastoral letter of April, 1969, the Archbishop of Havana, Emilio Díaz, said to the progressive Catholics of Latin America, "We denounce this unjust blockade which contributes to the increasing unnecessary suffering of the people and impedes the attempts to improve conditions. We appeal, therefore, to the conscience of those who are in a favorable position to take effective actions designed to put an end to the measure."

Disciples of Pope John, unconcerned by the "communist" label, heard the appeal from the Cuban Church. So did those who followed the precepts and example of the progressive attitudes of Paul VI who had just visited Uganda and was preparing to go to Hiroshima; who had not hesitated to carry on dialogue with the Soviet leaders; who had understood the student movement as a longing for sincerity, for justice, and for renewal; and who had congratulated Cuba in a message to President Osvaldo Dorticós on January, 1969, on the tenth anniversary of the Cuban revolution.

The Scientific *Aggiornamento*

Cuernavaca

A peaceful city, a city of arroyos and flowers. Hernán Cortés recognized all its assets. In order to enjoy the delightful climate, he had his palace constructed there of stones as smooth as though they had been cut with a knife. The Franciscans who arrived with him erected their monastery in 1529 in an ascetic architectural style which after four centuries is ennobled by the austerity of post-conciliar worship. Maximilian of Hapsburg, who was given to splendid blunders, cultivated gardens and romances there during the Mexican dream. Emiliano Zapata rode his white horse down those rock-paved streets shouting, "Land and Liberty."

In the luster of history and the shade of jacarandas, among thousands of unconcerned tourists and artisans skilled with the loom and brush, Cuernavaca again attracts the world's notice through the work of three erudite humanist priests of courage and simple, apostolic sincerity. This city of bouganvillae and hibiscus situated 73 kilometers from Mexico City is the epicenter of the scientific *aggiornamento* in the Latin American Church. It has tried to keep the Vatican Curia's eyes open but its ears closed to the monsignors of the Holy Office.

The Congregation for the Propagation of the Faith, the ancient Inquisition, watches Cuernavaca from Rome without confidence and with much prejudice, unable, however, to see the flowers that provide honey for the beehives. The Roman inquisitors know that on the other side of those fences blazing with color and those murmuring arroyos garnished with fruits and aromas a profound renovation of the Church is in progress. Three sensitive elements— priestly vocation, social research, and the liturgy—are being tested by revision which provokes, alternately, the anger of the Holy

Office and the benevolence of Paul VI. Innovations in these three areas have aroused conflicting emotions generally ranging from respect and admiration of the "Abrahamite" minorities, to use Helder Cámara's term, to the fury of those who resist religious utilization of modern processes of science, free examination in social investigation, and bringing the liturgy in touch with the popular classes.

Dom Gregoire Lemercier, Father Ivan Illich, and Bishop Sergio Méndez Arceo are renewing the traditional concepts of religious vocation, imaginative and interested consideration of the actual conditions in the continent, and are pointing out the fallacies of ostentatious worship which is indispensable to the professionals of aristocratic and esoteric pomp. All this has been occurring in a provincial Mexican city with a population of 50,000 which on weekends is tripled by an avalanche of visitors who come to enjoy themselves in the sensuality of its climate and scenery.

Psychoanalysis for Religious Vocation

What are the motives that influence a man to choose the religious life? Do all have equal validity? Are all equally effective for service to the Church and society integrally considered? Such questions troubled the intelligence and ethical sensibilities of a Belgian monk, Prior of the Benedictine Monastery of the Resurrection in Santa María Amacatitlan, situated among beautiful hills a dozen kilometers from Cuernavaca.

Dom Gregoire was not inventing anything. At the beginning of the century the Church accepted the confrontation of the old classical spiritualism with the concrete goals which modern science proposed from its laboratories in a renovating technical criticism. The great figure in that trend especially adjusted to the experimental psychology as opposed to spiritualist philosophy was the Belgian, Cardinal Desiderio J. Mercier. He considered absurd, contrary to human spirit and to its history, the refusal to comprehend the origin and the end of beings that our senses observe. A quarter of a century later, the wisdom of the Jesuit Pierre Teilhard de Chardin, with his theory concerning the evolution of man, tried to introduce scientific investigation in the field of ethnology into the Church.

When the encyclical *Aeterni Patris* of Pope Leo XIII indicated that Thomistic philosophy must take precedence in Catholic teaching, Mercier, who had just become a canon of the University of Louvain, assumed the task of preventing the Church, perplexed and turned inward, from remaining to one side of the scientific advances in the knowledge of man himself and the discoveries that were giving psychology a new dimension. Cardinal Mercier developed the University of Louvain into a center of modern Catholic thought. His book, *The Origins of Contemporary Psychology*, opened to the Church ample perspectives for integration with scientific thought and contemporary techniques. By the time of Cardinal Mercier's death in January, 1926, he had made contributions to the Church which would be very difficult to disregard in the future.

Twenty-six years later in a speech before the members of the International Congress of Psychotherapy and Clinical Psychology, Pius XII renewed the interest that Cardinal Mercier had initiated by saying,

Be sure that the Church follows with its warmest sympathy and most fervent prayers your research and your medical experiments. You are laboring in a very difficult field. Your activity, nevertheless, can produce valuable results for medicine, for a more profound understanding of the soul in general, and for the religious inclinations of man in his most complete development.

Would the possibilities that science offers be discarded? Would theology and science meet in definitive conflict? In applying psychoanalysis to religious life, the Church would have to overcome the obstacles and impediments of neuroses, sexual perversions, and various psychosomatic phenomena that some of its ministers imposed on it. The most frequent aberrations among the religious are: estrangement, separation, or unreality with respect to the body and the exterior world which Dugas in 1898 called depersonalization; the horror of sin transformed into anticipation of frightful events or fear of having committed mortal sin and being condemned to hell; paranoid states and flagellation; unreasoning fear of women and abnormally weak enunciation; deliriums and hallucinations in delicate temperaments that struggle with their destinies until they fall prey to magic and to the mystery of schizophrenia; and the melancholia of nuns at the menopause.

Not all religious have been truly called by God. Feigning is possible either consciously or unconsciously. Defective motives, psychologic distortions, false vocations which perturb and hinder the ecclesiastic life may be found among monks and postulates. It is not valid to generalize the concept—converting it into a doctrine—that any given person owes his vocation to a call by God, that the religious life is a charisma conceded from on high to certain privileged persons who as a consequence of that selection are obligated to dedicate themselves to the sanctification of their fellow men.

The moral and theological conflict of the Benedictine Prior of the Monastery of the Resurrection began to drift slowly toward an interior drama. In 1960 in a memorandum sent from Cuernavaca to the abbots of his order, Gregoire Lemercier asked, "How are our brothers, our monks recruited? . . . The only condition for entering the monastery is the one St. Benedict required—the search for God." Dom Gregoire's faith and his exacting concept of the priestly function collided each day with the grave psychological deviations of the religious under his direction and care. Infantilism, narcissism, and a varied repertory of neuroses afflicted not a few monks. Homosexuality had cast its shadow in the monastery. The Prior had vigorously confronted deviations and had struggled to deal with them. Resorting to measures available to him, he increased the work periods in the workshops and cultivated fields, he resorted to prayer, and at the same time sought to distract the fantasies of his brothers by cultivating original styles of religious imagery. His efforts were futile.

The Prior began to suspect that for some the search for God was a mirage, a self-deceit, an act of frustration by a life broken or wounded by subconscious problems, difficult or impossible to bring to the surface of consciousness for effective and adequate treatment.

How could the authenticity or falsity of the "interior vocation" which St. Ignatius had called for be discovered? How could that "right intention" of the Society of St. Sulpice which had become a rule of priestly vocation be made precise in order to avoid mistakes? The traditional Church indicated as negative signs for religious vocations some generalities which were more of a disciplinary or moral nature than psychological. But might not those negative signs be fictional, a false appearance, which an authentic vocation could correct? So might the positive signs—inclination to prayer and horror of sin—hide psychic ailments, cover up complexes, conceal frustrations. How can the personal universe submerged in the depths of the subconscious be detected in the postulant or seminarist?

The Abbot's inability to deal with such conflicts, which transcended his community, with traditional means deeply disturbed his conscience and became a nightmare of doubt about the purity of his own vocation. Some events raised questions about what he had once called, in firm conviction, "the balancing effect of the monastic life." A Mexican writer has recognized, in a notably documented conception, the internal anguish that would not let the Benedictine Prior of Cuernavaca rest. His fixed faith came into conflict in a lascerating struggle with what he personally saw in the monastery. Vicente Leñero in his work *Pueblo Rechazado (Rejected People)* attributed to Dom Gregoire the statement that, "I was born and created there, in the scenario more than the role; I was only the author. That is the truth. In it, I was at the point of terminating my whole life's work. . . . Leprosarium. Insane asylum. What was the use of my denying it? The ship sinks, my search is shipwrecked. . . . Why? What did I do wrong? Where was my error? Was it my folly? Was it pride? Was arrogance my sin?"

Let us note how Gregoire Lemercier himself described the outcome.

On the night of October 4, 1960, I was in bed, awake, lying on my back. Suddenly I saw before me myriad flashes of lightning in all colors. It was a supremely beautiful spectacle. My eyes were wide open, and I enjoyed inexpressibly those artificial fires which I should have liked to prolong indefinitely. I turned on my left side. Then, on the wall of my cell appeared something like a small screen on which I saw in rapid succession a series of human faces. As the kaleidoscope paused I saw a handsome countenance, one of supreme goodness. Immediately, I cried, "My God, why do you not speak to me?" At once I began to cry violently as I was filled with a profound consciousness of being loved by God. I wanted to tell him that I loved him, but that did not seem important to me. I wanted to tell him that he could do with me whatever he wanted, but I was afraid that he would not take me seriously. I felt profoundly that I did not merit that love on account of my sins. All was condensed in a feeling of defeat, of dominion of God over me, and, at the same time, of great joy. It lasted many hours. When I could not endure more, I telephoned an amateur psychologist who lived nearby to come and keep me company.

On the day following, fearing that I was losing my mind—I, a strong man, one of few words, cerebral, in no way inclined to the marvelous, extremely skeptical about any sort of mysticism or pseudo-mysticism—and on the advice of the amateur psychologist, consulted again the President of the Mexican Association of Psychoanalysis. Some months before he had deterred me from entering psychoanalysis. I now explained to him in detail all that had happened, giving him, moreover, data I had not given him before. After listening to me in silence, he said, simply, "I know your work in the monastery. In addition to your strong personality and the strength you derive from your religion, it would help you to have a more technical basis for meeting the problems you encounter in the monastery. Undergo psychoanalysis."

January 17, 1961, three months after receiving that advice, Prior Gregoire Lemercier began psychoanalysis. At that moment there began in Cuernavaca for many observers one of the most intense religious experiences of our century. The positive results that Dom Gregoire was able to recognize in himself induced him to suggest the same therapy to his brother monks, leaving them completely free to accept or reject his counsel. The majority agreed, and the life of the monastery was profoundly transformed. The Prior interrupted his treatment briefly to take advantage of the three opportunities he had to go to Rome as private expert to the Bishop of Cuernavaca, Sergio Méndez Arceo, in the deliberations of Vatican Council II. The Mexican bishop, aware of the results obtained by psychotherapy in the Monastery of the Resurrection, proposed in that assembly an open, unprejudiced study of the possibilities which the technique put at the disposition of the post-conciliar Church. Since Cardinal Mercier and then Pius XII had initiated the matter, the Church did not lack knowledge of the way to enter religious life that modern science made clear.

The commission of cardinals appointed to study the matter totally ignored the results that the Benedictines of Cuernavaca had obtained as well as the reports of Méndez Arceo at Vatican Council II, and even the above-mentioned address by Pius XII. On July 16, 1961 a *monitum* of the Holy Office condemned the experiment and warned that "the sacred edifice of the monastery could not be used for any Freudian experiment." The commission of cardinals ordered Dom Gregoire under pain of censure *a divini* to refrain from upholding, in public or private, the theories and practices of Sigmund Freud.

Discouragement spread in the Monastery of the Resurrection, and despair was prevalent in the most advanced scientific circles of Catholicism in Mexico and in the world. Dom Gregoire began to wonder even whether Pius XII, student of Cardinal Mercier, had actually been receptive to psychoanalysis in 1953.

A deluge of scandal and derision poured over the twenty-one monks (out of twenty-four) who supported Gregoire Lemercier. The press fed the public's morbidity with big headlines. In Paris *France Soir* exaggerated the issue by asking, "Is this a repetition of Galileo's case?" The chorus of Pharisees was quick to hurl denunciations at the monks, crying, "Mortal sin! Eternal damnation!"

The Prior and his disciples were not willing to give up psychoanalysis; neither did they intend to disobey Rome. Calmly they dressed in secular clothing, took their tools and books, hung their Benedictine habits in the closet, and sadly abandoned the Monastery of the Resurrection of Santa María Amacatitlan. Together they founded a new community of "plain Christians," then applied for return to lay status in accordance with the norms of Canon Law. It was a case of "fidelity to a personal vocation," the Bishop of Cuernavaca explained in accordance with his understanding of the action.

Gregoire Lemercier's life has seemed extraordinarily rich from his birth at Lieges to the time when he set up the foundation which he called the Emmaus Center of Psychoanalysis a few hundred meters from the Monastery of the Resurrection. (Emmaus: an example of the Christian apostolate. St. Luke refers to two of the Lord's disciples who, on the day of the Resurrection, were on their way to the village of Emmaus at the foot of the mountains of Judea when someone overtook them, asking them why they were so melancholy. They replied that the Master had died on the cross three days before. The man then expounded the Holy Scriptures to them and explained that it was right and proper for the Lord to suffer in order that he might redeem the world. The one who had overtaken them was Jesus.) Lemercier indicated that he had founded the Emmaus center because psychoanalytical treatment had been transformed by the western capitalistic system into a luxury which few can afford.

In his childhood he had dreamed of becoming a missionary. In his youth he studied theology at Louvain where the spirit of Cardinal Mercier was present. Liturgical reform attracted him. After serving as a chaplain in World War II, he was sent to Mexico to open a monastery. Without any intention on his part, his faith in God and his faith in science placed him, in Cuernavaca, in an equivocal position. He had hoped that the psychotherapies undertaken at the Monastery of the Resurrection would prompt the postconciliar Church to take a firm position regarding scientific advances in the face of anachronistic dogmatism and steril prejudices. The Holy Office—the Old Church—prevented it.

The Roman Congregation of Religious had known about the Benedictine Prior of Cuernavaca since 1963. The Superior Abbot of the Benedictine authorized the experiments the following year. The judgments of the Roman Congregation of Religious had favored them. But the Congregation for the Propagation of the Faith—the Holy Office—took a different position. When the matter came to its attention, it proceeded with haste and extreme severity. The Inquisition ordered Dom Gregoire, then in Rome, to return to Belgium, suspend all contacts with the Mexican monastery, and separate himself from the Bishop whom he had served as adviser. In the last instance Paul VI agreed to name a commission of cardinals to judge Lemercier's case. It followed the line of the Holy Office: its judgment was fulminating and final. The *beatos* jubilantly thundered that the Church does not modify its judgments.

But the Church did begin to make modifications. On February 1, 1969 the Vatican issued an instructive entitled *Renovationis Causam* with its elaboration entrusted to the Congregation of Religious Seculars. The document, which had Paul VI's prior approval, introduced innovations in monastic and pre-priestly life which, according to Catholic world opinion, would turn attention to the ruins of the abandoned Monastery of the Resurrection and the prosperous Psychoanalytic Center of Emmaus. According to that Vatican decree, young men and women who had made preliminary vows to follow a religious career could take as much time as they desired to test their vocations in the outside world, attend a university, and engage in work. The objective was to enable them to make free and responsible decisions about spending their lives in a religious order.

Had not Gregoire Lemercier proposed just that for the Benedictines of Cuernavaca? Having observed his ecclesiastical downfall, a theological friend had rightfully pointed out that he was ten years ahead of his time and then counseled him to continue to work in silence.

Were the situations that Dom Gregoire had faced in his monastery particularly difficult? In February, 1969 the Holy See had instructed that in certain difficult cases, religious superiors may resort to the services of a prudent and capable psychologist who is distinguished by his moral principles to help in determining whether a candidate for the priesthood can with propriety assume the obligations of the religious state. That was precisely what Lemercier had done in the Monastery of the Resurrection.

Was Prior Lemercier mistaken, perhaps, in his choice of a system? If the fact is accepted that psychotherapy is a treatment which activates the patient's spirit, body, or mind, or if a person in a different degree has a repressed personality, then it must be agreed that Dom Gregoire could only have taken recourse to the method of Sigmund Freud. Obviously, it has been improved in our time as all the sciences have. More than thirty years ago, Father

Gemelli, Rector and Professor of the Catholic University of Milan and President of the Academy of Sciences of the Vatican, stressed the need for approaching psychoanalysis as one of the most far-reaching conquests of our time.

In *Renovationis Causam* in February, 1969 the Holy See had said that the liberty accorded those who had taken their first vows to leave their convents and seminaries and return to worldly life would be without a time limit. The Vatican was endeavoring to reduce the desertion of priests by avoiding the entry into religious life of those lacking a firm vocation. It announced that it desired to undertake an experiment on a large scale to modernize the methods for determining who should be priests and nuns and to give aspirants the opportunity to determine their lives freely.

Six months after these instructions had been issued in Rome, José Álvarez Barroni, Rector of the Conciliar Seminary in Mexico, and Dr. José de Jesús González, psychotherapist of the institution, arranged a press conference to release the information that for five years they had used clinical interviews, both superficial and profound, depending on the personality of the subject, psychological tests to find out the interests, aptitudes, and personality of the seminarist, examinations designed to improve the selection of candidates, noting that these analyses were made yearly during the time the seminarist remained in the institution. According to Father Álvarez Barroni and Dr. González, the results were eminently satisfactory. They said, "We now work with a group of students mentally sound who have true vocations for the priesthood."

Dr. Santiago Campero, priest-secretary of the Conference of Religious Institutes of Mexico, indicated the eclectic position of the hierarchy when he declared that the Church did not prohibit psychoanalysis; neither had it regressed in the decision of the Holy See regarding the case of Gregoire Lemercier. The desirable objective, he explained, was to avoid the abuse of that technique for inducing or revealing the priestly or religious vocation.

Galileo had to wait four hundred years. The monks of the Monastery of the Resurrection did not have that much patience. The Emmaus group continued, ingeniously and effectively, dedicated to the apprenticeship of happiness. All were up at dawn to work eight hours daily in the woodworking, carpentry, printing, serigraphy, and ceramics shops. They took part in group direction of the Center and practiced psychotherapy. They admitted men of any race or creed. At the University of Upsala in East Orange, New Jersey, Gregoire Lemercier declared, with reason, that "the day will come in which this will be the usual procedure, and priests of the future will not be judges of conscience but its promoters." His opinion coincided with that of the most authoritative religious and psychiatric centers of the world.

The Vatican has not resolved a frank *aggiornamento* between theology and science by means of contemporary techniques. In this instance, it seems that the Vatican has lacked an intelligence as profound and fresh as that of Cardinal Desiderio J. Mercier at the beginning of the century.

Social Research Without Dogmatism

The priest Ivan Illich founded the Intercultural Documentary Center *(Centro Intercultural de Documentación—*CIDOC) in Cuernavaca with the permission of his diocesan superior, the Archbishop of New York, Cardinal Francis Spellman. Within his jurisdiction, Bishop Sergio Méndez Arceo of Cuernavaca offered him ample backing. He was aware that Father Illich, born in Vienna on September 4, 1927, had studied advanced natural science in Florence, that he had received a doctorate from the Austrian University in Salzburg with specialization in nineteenth century philosophy of history, that he had received a degree in philosophy and theology from the Gregorian University in Rome, and that he was an alumnus of Capranico, also in Rome. Moreover, John XXIII had given him the title of secret chamberlain to the pontiff and also made him a monsignor.

The Center holds classes in Spanish for about one hundred resident foreigners in the city. Some speak French but most of them English. About twenty are linked in some way with Catholic or Protestant organizations. Some 15 percent of the students are priests and nuns, and twenty-four are Protestant missionaries from the United States. In Emmaus, a few kilometers distant, the lecture halls bear the names of discoverers and developers of psychoanalysis—Freud, Jung, Adler—while at the Center they are known by the simple pictures that adorn the walls: Flower Hall, Hall of Birds, Hall of Globes, Hall of Ships. The library is especially rich in works about the changes occurring in Latin America. The Center offers to professors from the United States and Europe courses on the culture and vital problems of the countries in this hemisphere. Its press has published many works on social and ideological changes in that area. After the Holy Office had vented its wrath and had acted arbitrarily against the institution, Bishop Méndez Arceo stated in a pastoral letter in June, 1969 that "With regard to CIDOC, we know that this Center and the associated institutions constitute a non-ecclesiastical community, an important object of our pastoral ministry, which has become integrated into the life of Cuernavaca as much in the temporal community as in the Christian, with incalculable benefits from an uninterrupted and attracting reflection about the realities of Latin America."

The Center also publishes basic sociological data concerning the region as a service to almost a hundred foreign libraries. The press contributes to the maintenance of the Institute along with subscriptions and monthly payments by students and participants.

Who could have foretold that at the height of the *aggiornamento* a ferocious storm would break loose on that community in Cuernavaca, on that small area of beautiful gardens surrounding a large white house? The first hurricane-like winds left no doubt about its force.

A characteristic of the Center has been freedom from imposition of conditions on teaching, on participation in its seminars and collaboration in its publications, or on the ideological or political connection of its professors, lecturers, or writers. Naturally, free research and authentic, objective investigation without pre-conditions are guaranteed by the participation of varied philosophical tendencies, ranging from scholastic to Marxian.

Among the participants in academic endeavors of teaching and research there are, naturally, some intellectuals who assume or maintain radical positions on diverse matters, including the religious. Father Illich has said that "In this place we let the imagination fly. Here no one pays us to think; consequently we think freely."

The studies of the Center with explicable, pains-taking, natural prolixity, concentrate on the conditions of poverty among the great majority of Latin Americans. How else can researchers as professional as these draw near the explosive ferment that threatens the economic, social, and political institutions of Latin America?

That provides the explanation for the displeasure, suspicion, and fury—in that order—which have fallen on CIDOC from the very first. Who benefits from the dissemination of the truth? The truth about Latin America—so the argument goes—profits only the agitators. And those everlasting communists who manipulate them. Determined bishops of the Old Church, the most typical and influential reactionary elements of the Latin American Church among both ecclesiastics and laity, initiated an increasingly intense campaign against this institute of outstanding teaching.

The president himself of the Conference of the Latin American Episcopate *(Conferencia del Episcopado Latinoamericana—* CELAM), the Brazilian Bishop Avelar Brandao, became interested in the problem. Not wanting to rely on unfounded rumors, he sent to Cuernavaca two theologians, Gera, an Argentinian, and Padin, a Brazilian. Under the auspices of CELAM they personally interviewed Father Illich and became acquainted with the Center's activities. The two clerics made their report which Avelar Brandao transmitted to Rome. Four months later he wrote Father Illich from Rome, "I arrived too late, and even though I was permitted to discuss the matter, they had already taken a definite stand."

Early in 1968 after a cruel and arbitrary trial, the Congregation for the Propagation of the Faith let loose its thunder and lightning on the CIDOC through its academic director, Father Ivan Illich.

The matters which have concerned Illich in Cuernavaca had previously aroused his intellectual uneasiness. He had worked in New York from 1951 to 1956 in a miserable parish of Puerto Rican immigrants. Then Cardinal Francis Spellman named him

Vice-Rector of the University of Ponce in Puerto Rico. There he made observations about problems of Latin Americans which his later investigations in Cuernavaca confirmed. He had insisted that the Puerto Ricans hold on to their historical and cultural heritage and that they speak Spanish. At that time he began to make himself suspect.

Afterwards in Mexico he wrote regarding the role that the Old Church played that,

> The human material and the money which was sent with strange motives brought with it an alien image of Christianity, a foreign concept of pastoral functions, and a foreign political message. It carried marks of North American capitalism of the 1950's. . . . This type of foreign generosity has tempted the Latin American Church even to the point of converting itself into a satellite of the cultural and political phenomenon of the North Atlantic. . . . Once more the Church is flourishing, but with the stigma imposed by the renewed Conquest—a plant nourished from afar. . . . Within these realities, the North American missionary assumed the traditional role of a lackey-chaplain of a colonial power. The dangers which implicitly accompany the use by the Church of foreign money assume the proportions of a caricature when a *gringo priest* administers the aid in order to silence the people of *underdeveloped* countries.

By 1962 some Catholic organizations in the United States, infected by the Kennedy literature, began to organize something on the order of an Alliance of Progress for the Church. They initiated a campaign for 20,000 volunteers with posters showing a pointing finger and a slogan stating that "Latin America needs YOU," and with allusions to the necessity for excoriating the "red menace." The augmentation of the Vietnam war evoked renewed political and psychological stimulus for the plan. A generation accustomed to intervention in Southeast Asia in order to impose its ideas and way of life with arms and money felt it had the same obligation in Latin America. Five years later, in the January 21, 1967 issue of the American Jesuit review, *America*, Father Illich evaluated the program. Even before he had called attention in Cuernavaca to the matter, he noted that

As Fr. Berrigan suggests, the rich and the powerful can decide not to give; the poor can hardly refuse to accept. Since almsgiving conditions the beggar's mind, the Latin American bishops are not entirely at fault in asking for misdirected and harmful foreign aid. A large measure of the blame lies with the underdeveloped ecclesiology of U.S. clerics who direct the "sale" of American good intentions.

Father Illich had left Puerto Rico with his senses sharpened. His difficulties began in 1956 when Spellman named him Vice-Rector of the Catholic University of Ponce. Four years after his arrival on the island, Bishop James McManus attempted to discourage Catholics from voting for a candidate for governor supported by the Free State Society. He sustained his action with the argument that the candidate was in favor of artificial methods of birth control. He tried to constrain them to vote for a party which he himself had organized which had as its symbol a papal banner with a rosary placed across it. Illich read the letter of the Bishop of Ponce to his colleagues in such a way that a wave of hilarity swept over the audience. That was all the colonial zeal of the Puerto Rican hierarchy needed to force him to leave the island. Immediately the Department of Political Science of Fordham University offered him a professorship in sociology in the Graduate School in conjunction with the Jesuit Joseph Fitzpatrick. Ivan Illich was then in charge of that seminar at Fordham.

In Cuernavaca Illich did not hide his conclusions based on detailed study and personal experience. He upheld the necessity for avoiding the importation of foreign institutions into Latin American education, public health services, and the Church itself. He called attention to the contrast between the marginal activities of official institutions and the activities of Latin American majorities marginally involved in official institutions.

The Latin American school aroused Father Illich's scientific curiosity. He saw in its imperfections the sources of many evils, concluding definitively that "It is an old and fat sacred cow. . . . For Latin American countries which lack large amounts of capital, it becomes a costly luxury which produces very little." Illich supported his contention with figures. According to the latest available censuses (1965–1966), not more than 30 percent of the students in any Latin American country who finished their elementary education were able to continue their studies. Father Pedro Arrupe, General of the Society of Jesus, who visited Latin America in 1969, recognized the actual situation. In his opinion the charge that Jesuits provide a classical education was justified. The "Black Pope" recognized that their schools ought to be open to everyone—to those who could and those who could not pay.

Especially in military regimes, Father Illich pointed out, interest had increased in retaining children in schools longer. Why? He argued forcefully that the procedure hid a perverse purpose. Between the ages of five and six, the child is taught that he *who knows more is worth more*. Only some will be able to remain in school. The great majority who cannot, generally for economic reasons, learn to respect that elite which can continue its education. The Latin American school, through this subtle psychological mechanism, creates a privileged group and teaches the masses to respect them. If, moreover, notice is taken that all governments have spread the idea that they provide free education, then that fallacy augments the propagation in the masses of a guilt complex which leads them to regard the elite with even more respect. In short, such education is an instrument for obtaining submission.

Through three successive stages the school preserves the bourgeois monopolies: it provides custody of children which eliminates from competency in work or politics those not benefited by that custody; it selects and provides the qualifications for success for a small minority—automatically discriminating against and marking for the rest of their lives the great majority; and it "indoctrinates" them; that is, it introduces the child to the values and ideologies of the groups which hold power.

Father Illich called attention to an oppressive force indicated by the following data: half the children in Latin America between the ages of six and fourteen, about thirty-five million, did not have access to primary schools; of seventy million adolescents, scarcely seven or eight million attended secondary schools, according to data supplied in August, 1969 by Gonzalo Abad Grijalva, Director of the Regional Center of School Construction in Latin America. How many of those seven or eight million attained a university education?

In Cuernavaca Illich concerned himself with matters even more obviously difficult. What will the Church be like in the society of the future which is approaching with sidereal velocity? He wrote for an Argentine review that

the basic unit of the Church of tomorrow will be a married man who earns his living independently of the Church and receives religious orders as an adult. A lay adult, ordained to the deaconate, will preside over the normal Christian community of the future. The ministry will be an exercise in his free time rather than a work. . . . The deacon will be a man mature in Christian learning acquired throughout his life in the bosom of an intimate liturgy, not a professional graduate of a seminary shaped by theological formulas. Often marriage and the rearing of children, and not the acceptance of celibacy as a legal condition of ordination, will give him the capacity for reasonable leadership.

For that society to which we look forward and which scientific advances are creating with vertiginous rapidity, Illich foretold that "the deaconry will be the primary institutional unity of the Church supplementing the parish. Its base will be the home rather than the Church."

In this case Illich neither invaded territory prohibited by the Church nor one foreign to its conciliar anxieties and meditations. The Belgian Cardinal Leo Joseph Suenens had concerned himself with the doctrinal bases of the deaconship, fixing its splendid historical roots and determining the conclusions of Vatican Council II in that respect:

The Council approached the problem and resolved it, as is known, accepting the restoration of a permanent deaconship accessible also to married men. This decision was taken, without doubt, for pastoral reasons; but not only on that account. The restoration of the permanent deaconship is declared and fundamentally justified by virtue of the sacramental character of the deaconship itself. In the Council, I tried to give the doctrinal justification of this return to tradition. Here is the essence of that attempt: Who opposes the restoration of the permanent deaconship forgets, it seems, that this question concerns the very constitution of the Church. This position is not dictated to us by some practical reality, but is supported by a supernatural realism founded in the faith on the sacramental character of the deaconship. I do not want to take sides on the questions debated today, especially the matter of the interpretation which may be given to the biblical fragment which refers to the election of Stephen and the other six deacons (Acts 6:3–6). Nevertheless, some data are firm, following clearly from the New Testament, from the first apostolic fathers (above all Clement of Rome and Ignatius of Antioquia), from later uninterrupted tradition, and from liturgical books, oriental as well as occidental. From the apostolic and subapostolic Church, some of the divine favors of the sacred ministry are attributed, according to a special and stable manner, to a rank distinct from that of the priest.

Yet in that moment, Illich held the view that the clergy was a decadent institution in the Church. He explained that

The Roman Church is the greatest non-governmental bureaucratic organization in the world. It employs a million eight hundred thousand full time workers, priests, brothers, and religious laymen. Those *employees* work within a corporate structure that has been considered by a North American consulting agency as one of the most efficiently directed organizations in the world. . . . This well-known fact is at times viewed with pride by some. For others, however, that same effective functioning of the machine is looked upon as reason for discredit. Some men suspect that the institutional Church has lost its significance before the world. Vacillation, doubt, and confusion prevail among its directors, functionaries, and employees. The giant begins to falter before it collapses.

Illich suggested that we would receive with a spirit of profound happiness the disappearance of institutional bureaucracy within the Church. Are the monsignori of the Roman Curia going to allow it?

The bureaucracy of the institutional Church was ready to show its claws. Illich's reflections about the Old and the New Church— about the Church of the past and the Church of the future—have stirred up many animosities. Francis Spellman was urged to summon him to his New York diocese; the Cardinal did not find that the solicitation merited his attention. At his death, Maguire, his successor, acquiesced, explaining that it was an order from the Vatican, under pain of censure. In effect, the Congregation for the Propagation of the Faith had summoned Father Illich to Rome.

On the left of the Basilica of St. Peter, viewed from the front, stands the structure housing the Holy Office where Father Illich was summoned on June 17, 1968. He was conducted to a subterranean chamber through a pair of double doors; the leather-covered inner pair was soundproof. He was left alone in a great hall. After a few minutes, Cardinal Franjo Seper, President of the Congregation for the Propagation of the Faith, appeared and extended his ring for the ritual kiss and cordially gave him his hand. Monsignor Luigi de Magistris conducted him from the hall by various short staircases to an office with a heavy table in the center. Seated and waiting for him was Giuseppe Casoria, theologian of the Holy Office who held also several other offices in the extensive Roman Curia. Illich approached the prelate. The dialogue was short and trenchant.

"I am Illich."

"I know that."

"Monsignor, who are you?"

"Your judge."

"I thought you would tell me your name."

"That is unimportant. I am Casoria."

De Magistris, Casoria, and Illich crossed themselves. The case had commenced. The accused insisted that he would not reply to any questions, disadvantaged as he was by not having received a copy of the charges against him. After forty-five minutes, the inquisitors agreed to provide him at 3:00 that afternoon with the accusations. He would be expected to return two hours later. They sent a copy of the charges to him at the Capranico College where he was staying and where he had studied from 1945 to 1951.

One general accusation and eighty-five questions were formulated in the interrogation which the inquisitors had drawn up. They called on him to answer a confused and malicious series of demands about his ideas and personal relations. Some of the latter implicated names of well-known religious and political personages and intellectuals. The general accusation and questions had been the subject of extensive study by canonists and jurists. One was enough. In its edition of February 15, 1969 the Jesuit review of the United States, *America*, carried an analysis of the treatment to which the Congregation for the Propagation of the Faith had subjected Father Illich. Regarding the questionnaire, Ladislas M. Orsay, graduate of the Honors School of Jurisprudence of Oxford University and Doctor of Canon Law, held that,

The headings are carefully worded and convey a strong intimation of guilt. . . .
While common law presumes a person to be innocent unless he is proved guilty, in this questionnaire guilt is strongly suggested. . . . [T]he formulation of many questions represents not only a medieval jurisprudence but a poor theology. . . .
The compiler of the questionnaire praises himself for "human understanding and priestly zeal," yet he puts the accused into a situation that is inconsistent with both justice and charity. . . . [W]hen the questionnaire is examined from the point of view of procedure, little difference can be found between it and the ones used in fairly well-known inquisitorial procedures.

From that incredible interrogation, as the Mexican Bishop Sergio Méndez Arceo described it, the following extracts may serve as examples:

Is it true that in 1960, influenced in a definitive way by the Benedictine monk and psychoanalyst, P. Lemercier, and with the unconditional support of the Bishop of Cuernavaca, Monsignor Méndez Arceo, there took place in you—treating and being treated as invested with divine gifts of favor—a dangerous general development of new ideas and dissolvent tendencies, humanistic and liberal, in prejudice of doctrine, tradition, and ecclesiastical discipline?
What can you reply to one who represents you as *restless, adventurous, imprudent, fanatic, and hypnotizing, rebellious toward all authority and disposed to accept and recognize only the diocesan Bishop of Cuernavaca?*
Is it a fact that in the establishments of CIF and CIDOC there are frequent gatherings and entertainments in the private quarters

of the young girls, guests, or employees which priests and nuns often attend?

Why, how, and when did your cultural and friendly relations with well-known heads and leaders of international political movements begin, especially those with Louis Alberto Gómez de Souza and the late Che Guevara?

Of what religious, political, and social nature were, and perhaps still are, your personal relations with the following Mexicans: Alfredo Cepeda, Horacio Flores de la Peña, Víctor Flores Olea, Carlos Fuentes, Leopoldo González Casanova, Vicente Lombardo Toledano, Mario Menéndez Rodríguez, Octavio Paz, and Luis Suárez?

How do you judge morally the clamorous deviation of the prominent Camilo Torres Restrepo? And why do you think the Church was wrong in denouncing him for his bellicose and revolutionary ideas?

On what grounds and for what reasons does Thomas R. Melville, apostate from religion, implicated in guerilla activities in Guatemala, make use of CIDOC in order to defend his apostacy and reply with impunity to the canonical censures of his superior general?

What is your opinion of modern priests, revolutionaries, and Latin American guerillas who hold that if a Catholic is not on the side of the revolutionaries, he is in mortal sin?

Is it a fact that, according to you, the Catholic Church is a mixture of superstition and anarchy and a supermarket of benefits which works only for money in order to protect priests and the religious, that it baptizes children wrongfully, obliges the faithful to attend communion often, favors the devotion of the Virgin and the saints, and demands frequent and repeated alms?

Is it a fact that you have been a part of the State Commission in Puerto Rico for birth control and that you counsel and recommend to your parishioners and in your conversations with lay persons and friends the use of contraceptive pills?

Do you also believe, how and why—making your own the calumny of others—, that the head of the Catholic Church lives in a sumptuous palace of a thousand rooms?

Why do you call the Catholic Church *an aristocrat who gives alms*, and what do you think and how do you interpret the missionary work of the Church at present and in the past?

What do you understand by *ecclesiastical bureaucracy* and why have you called the Church *God's Business* and *the Lord's Supermarket?*

Is it a fact that you are opposed to *ecclesiastical celibacy* as much for the clergy as for the religious? How do you judge the methods of applying psychoanalysis to clerical and religious vocations?

Is it a fact that you have compared convents and religious houses with concentration camps of personality destruction and forced labor? And that you want admitted to them only the timid, the old, the sick, and the infirm?

Is it true that for you, priests and nuns who are faithful to communism and to Castro are witnesses for Christ, while the rest have dedicated themselves heretofore, or still do, to taking from their companions, the rich?

Is it true that you are accustomed to make pronouncements about the clergy of today and tomorrow, with respect to the coming of a new order of religious and social aid for the world which will cleanse all the structures of the ancient, traditional order?

Is it true that in Cuernavaca that many oddities are permitted and that celebrations and concelebrations of the Mass are carried out without soutanes and in shirt sleeves?

Is it true that you want to allow women to confess without the *reja* of the confessional?

Father Ivan Illich felt that he could not answer in two hours a questionnaire so extensive as that, and one, moreover, propounded on such an inquisitorial basis. He wrote Cardinal Seper, "This is carried to the point of formulating some questions in such a way as apparently to call on me . . . to implicate or accuse some friends and confreres, indeed even the Bishop of the diocese in which I live and work." He renewed his full and unconditional profession of faith as a Catholic. He delivered the manuscript the following day to Cardinal Seper himself, who interrupted the interview to say to him in Croatian, *"Hajdite, hajdite, nemojte se vratiti."* (Get going, get going, and do not come back.)

After leaving, while he was still in St. Peter's Square, Ivan Illich pondered the fact that Cardinal Seper, Head of the Holy Office, had repeated the last words which the Grand Inquisitor in Dostoyevski's *The Brothers Karamazov* had said to his prisoner.

Within the year, Giuseppe Casoria was promoted in the Vatican bureaucracy. Because of his accomplishments and merits demonstrated in the inquisitorial process of Ivan Illich, he was advanced to the subsecretariat attached to the Congregation for the Discipline of the Sacraments. The rewards that the Holy Office might have derived from Father Illich's case have not been universally recognized. For example, Catholics who attended the International Conference on Human Rights in New York in January, 1969 characterized the Vatican's action against the CIDOC as reactionary and the process against its academic director as monstrous.

In Cuernavaca Bishop Sergio Méndez Arceo received on January 18, 1969, the proscription of CIDOC issued by the Congregation for the Propagation of the Faith. The bearer, Monsignor Guido del Mestri, Apostolic Delegate to Mexico, rushed into the Center with it. Ivan Illich wrote to his diocesan superior that

I have decided to renounce definitively all exercise of the privileges and powers that the Church conferred on me. . . . In these last months and years my love for the Holy Roman Church has given me greater sensitivity and depth. Help me to give witness to those attitudes; to my absolute and rigorous submission to doctrinal authorities . . . with all their limitations, weaknesses, and anachronisms which may characterize them . . . ; of my love for the Church as it is, because in its historical aspects I recognize the only properly sacramental presence of the Lord among us; of my acceptance of the Canon Law of the Roman Church. . . . It is my desire to contribute also to the profound renewal of the Holy Church.

CIDOC continued its research activities. But the *aggiornamento* had ended for Father Illich. He continued his studies in his lay status, respected by the professors and students of different religious creeds and nationalities, ever more numerous in the classrooms in one of the many large, dazzlingly white houses on the outskirts of Cuernavaca. In a pastoral letter to his parishioners, Bishop Méndez Arceo indicated that Father Illich's presence in the Christian community gives him happiness and hope and gives us the riches of his extraordinary personality.

Science and History

If the Brazilian Bishop Helder Cámara in Recife represented the *aggiornamento* of the Latin American Church in social sciences, Sergio Méndez Arceo, Bishop of Cuernavaca, has been the learned explorer in science and in the liturgy for the Young Church of this hemisphere. His contributions to Vatican Council II were in plans for making the liturgy an expression, with austerity and joy, of the people. His Pan American Sunday Mass in the Cathedral at Cuernavaca with the earthy severity of its ornaments, the way in which the community of the faithful entered into the ceremony, the exhilarating melodies—the people liked the mariachis, "La Adelita," the *"Son de la Negra,"* and *"El Siete Leguas"* of the *villistas*—indicated the way to make the people feel included in the Church, and how, with humility, affection, and good sense, it could keep wide open an approach to peasants and urban workers. The sincere charity of the primitive Church, free of affectations and sectarian rigidities, was put into practice in the Cuernavaca diocese, without fear or prejudice, through a loving interpretation of what the Young Church in the post-conciliar era ought to be.

The Mexican Church was called on to follow suit. A few days after the announcement of the plans for construction of a new, immense, and sumptuous Basilica of Guadalupe, the greatest shrine of Mexican Catholicism, to replace the present one which is threatened with collapse, the Bishop of Cuernavaca expressed his opposition in the Mexico City newspaper *Excélsior* on October 12, 1969:

The aforesaid announcement is at first view a challenge to clear Christian conscience, even to the good sense of the man in the street. . . . One such enormous edifice would be just the opposite of the pastoral shrines which, happily, are being started in various places in the Republic, though not yet at the most-visited shrine of the country. To make one such expensive edifice for use during the few days of the year when it is so densely crowded would be a luxury offensive to the poverty of the immense majority of the pilgrims who could feel themselves comforted only through psychological transports.

Méndez Arceo had tasted bitter draughts. The Benedictine Lemercier had been his assistant with respect to psychoanalytical matters during the sessions of Vatican Council II. In full Council, the Bishop of Cuernavaca publicly affirmed that if the Church wants a sincere and loyal dialogue with the man of our time, it cannot ignore the genuine analysts. Psychoanalysis possesses a force which can afford great help to men in whom faith is mixed with psychological deviations which are disfiguring and inhibiting. With respect to the silence of Schema XIII (The Church in the Modern World), Méndez Arceo wrote on September, 1963, "Our text considers changes in the world in all categories—scientific, technical, economic, and other revolutionary developments. But why does it say nothing about the psychological revolution tied so closely to the conformation of the faith?"

The fulminations against Dom Gregoire Lemercier and his monks endowed the Bishop of Cuernavaca with sufficient spiritual clarity to say that those who had left the order were worthy of

respect due our brothers even though we are not in agreement with them. Their resignations are the means by which they seek to pursue their experiment by which they conscientiously believe they can contribute to the well-being of the world, the monastic state, and the Church. They cannot do it as priests and religious, but as laymen. That monastery had constituted a center irradiating Christian life through its efforts to renew Benedictine monasticism, giving outstanding notice of what is being accomplished at this time: their life of poverty, of peace, of work, of benefactions, of charity.

Because the vigorous and clear-headed Bishop kept up with social changes in Latin America, he supported Ivan Illich. Since he knew the plight of the humble classes in Latin America as well as Helder Cámara, he, too, was distressed by them. He declared that, "I understand perfectly those who believe that only armed violence can counteract the violence of the oppressors." The word of Christ, in his opinion, is still explosive. In the middle of a Mass he embraced Ivan Illich, for both believed that in every man there is something of Christ, be he Protestant or Catholic, patient of Freud, or a believer in Marx or Marcuse.

His churchly dignity outraged by the Holy Office, in Paul VI's presence the Bishop appealed to the Holy See to amend the error committed against the CIDOC. Paul VI indicated his willingness to withdraw the hastily issued prohibition made in his name against the priests and religious who frequented the Center and manifested also his concern for Father Illich who would not be required to leave Cuernavaca immediately. The Bishop, however, would be charged with the pastoral task of procuring Father Illich's fidelity to his priestly vocation. Also an immediate indication of confidence from the Pope to the Bishop of Cuernavaca would be made.

A papal disauthorization of the Vatican Curia did not seem possible in spite of everything. Many situations raise the suspicion that the pontifical bureaucracies maintain a heavy curtain—prejudice, fear, and ignorance of reality—around the Supreme Pontiff in order to immobilize the *aggiornamento* in Latin America.

Under the inquisitorial vigilance of the Congregation for the Propagation of the Faith, to which he had refused to respond because he would render account only to the Pope, Méndez Arceo compared his relations with Cuernavaca to the affinity in a marriage. He confessed, "I, the husband, allow the diocese to influence me and I influence it. But I can never say that we have arrived at a perfect understanding. That would be to lie. Cuernavaca and I carry on our search together; we are always traveling the same road." That would be, likewise, a good description of the relations of the Mexican Church—one of the youngest, nationally, in Latin America—with the State and with society as soon as history had delimited the scope of the two powers, for the Reform with Benito Juárez in the past century and the Revolution in this century had subtly improved those relations through the long, irreversible practice of those liberal principles which today form a part of the nation's character by general consent.

On March 26, 1968 the Mexican episcopate issued a Pastoral Letter on the development and unity of the country, endorsed by seventy-eight bishops, the apostolic prefect, and two of the apostolic administrators, headed by Cardinal José Garibi Rivera, Archbishop of Guadalajara, to mark the first anniversary of the encyclical *Populorum Progressio*. It expressed new views regarding the pastoral mission of the hierarchy within the context of the current situation in Mexico. In the part entitled "Attitude toward Reality," the hierarchy stated,

We must, above all, recognize that our country presents encouraging signs of progress in a variety of ways: cultural (reduction of illiteracy, increased access of the population to education, scientific and technical advances, and very appropriate cultural manifestations); economic (growth of national production, greater productivity, expansion of markets, investments, consumption, and of communications, etc); social (greater sense of organization and solidarity, growth of the middle class, etc.); civic-political (overcoming of fratricidal rivalries, greater consciousness and participation, improved dialogue); international (the country recognized for its attachment to what is right, to reason, to fraternal association, to mutual respect, etc.); and in other diverse ways which reveal the force of large numbers of our compatriots in spheres of public life or in the quiet of ordinary activities. All these form a new type of heroism and good citizenship; that of fulfilling daily responsibilities and duties.

Nevertheless, that same Pastoral Letter showed that with respect to the internal life of the Church there still remained some anachronisms in the institutional Church which were understood and expressed in a limited way by the hierarchy's dictation. The preceding did not prevent the Mexican bishops in treating the theme of the Church in the World from making clear that they understood by the world "the whole human family with the entire range of circumstances in which they live," in agreement with the pastotal constitution *Gaudiam Spes* on the Church and world of today, also pointing out that the Church is not juxtaposed to the world; it is in the world.

The foregoing acknowledgment reached the hierarchy in the third week of August, 1969 when an assembly of bishops, priests, religious, and laymen met at the Mission Seminary to consider the Mexican pastoral documents and those of the Latin American Episcopal Conference of Medellín, Colombia (CELAM). It was an ecclesiastical, not solely an episcopal meeting. Participating were sixty bishops and about a hundred laymen—technicians and professionals—all interested in relating the Church to currents of modern thought and in the process serving social changes without invading areas belonging to the temporal power. The attention to the local church through the participation by all sectors of the Church indicated a really promising beginning. The circumstances in which priest and layman were able in the presence of bishops to speak the truth as they saw it constituted the first step of a genuine reform in the internal structure of the Mexican Church. The customs and delays specifically noted could be attributed to the inertia which obstructs mental change. Designating causes and effects was an indication of reform which all sectors approved. The assembly at the Mission Seminary, logical consequence and intelligent outcome of the Pastoral Letter of March, 1968, clearly showed that the Mexican Church—if the scientific *aggiornamentos* which had been undertaken in Cuernavaca were not enough—was awake and young.

Sharp wit and youthfulness beset to good effect a graduate of the Medical School of the National Autonomous University of Mexico. He became an active, social, and struggling parish priest of Magdalena Mixhuca, a slum on the outskirts of Mexico City, set off by its misery. The priest, Juan Salazar Green, doctor of psychology and expert theologian since his ordination in 1963, sought to bring light to a critical reality by pointing out that "People of Mexico do not know how to make confession. Confessions are used to tell lies, to recount the family disputes or admit dishonest relations or prohibited sexual practices; but Catholics still do not know how to make a confession which covers the Ten Commandments and the five precepts of the Catholic Church." His pastoral sincerity had resulted in his being moved seven times in the six years he had exercised his priestly vocation in other parishes. What are the exact relations of urban people to the Church? Father Salazar thought that,

The juridical concept of the parish, considered as a portion of territory received from the bishop for spiritual guidance of the people and for pastoral labor to bring souls to salvation, is not now functional since it is not in accord with reality. In fact only persons who live very near the church attend it to take part in liturgical ceremonies celebrated there. Then there are those who come to the parish church through obligation because they must be baptized to be able to contract a marriage or because a minor must be baptized.

Father Salazar Green struggled alone against the superstitious ideas of his parishioners, against the subtle distortions of the faith, against vital deficiencies. His valor in speaking out freely led to his transfers. For example, he stated that, "Many faithful attributed supernatural cause to that which clearly originates from a perfectly natural cause. They ask the Lord to cure a child of dysentery when what they ought to do is improve personal and domestic hygiene."

No one can give assurance that Magdalena Mixhuca will be able to retain the medical assistance which Father Salazar had provided through the organization of a dispensary in charge of a doctor and several assistants, and the organization which provided employment for desperately needy persons. Had the upper level of the hierarchy in the Federal District of Mexico favored, ignored, or been antagonistic to this doctor-cleric's efforts?

Another case reflects the insensible struggle between the Young Church and the decrepit rigidity of certain prelates in provincial Mexico. A young priest, Mariano Amaya Serrano, was a professor of sociology, statistics, and law in the University of Querétaro which is one of the most progressive in the country, compatible with the history of that city which witnessed the collapse of the French empire in the last century and the birth of the Constitution of 1917. In those cloisters Father Amaya found something he had to learn: "My relations with students in Querétaro have helped me to practice Christianity in a way different from that of the fathers of old." He applied the new practices to his Masses in La Merced Chapel which many lively and enthusiastic students attended every Sunday. "Pop" and "go-go" music accompanied Father Amaya's Masses. When his colleagues in the city chided him, he responded, "Why do you take from your neighbor? Why don't you work as I do? Why don't you stop using the churches as a source of income?"

The Bishop of Querétaro, Alfonso Toriz Cobián, entered the dispute with all the weight of his authority when Father Amaya criticized the silent procession of Holy Week which had been held in the city each of the preceding three years. Wearing hoods, the rich people of Querétaro led the procession with the humble people following. Bishop Toriz Cobián collected 150 *pesos* from each person for permission to march in the parade. In Amaya's opinion that procession was nothing more than a social occasion, a religious pantomime. He labeled the priests who sponsored it masochists, and reproached the bishop for making it a commercial venture. In unison the clerics of the Querétaran diocese lashed out at Father Amaya. The Bishop ordered him expelled from La Merced Chapel. The students occupied the Chapel and roamed the streets in defense of their teacher. Toriz Cobián yielded to the students to suppress the conflict. As soon as the students were distracted, the priest Juan Berumen made false declarations against Father Amaya, against his social work and his liturgical tendencies. But the Querétaran students were ready to confront their irresolute Bishop of the Old Church who was incapable of comprehending the public confession of the priest of La Merced, who said, "I, myself, bought the musical instruments because I thought that modern music has something of the mystical in it." Was it another heresy like that of the two in Cuernavaca, but one without a postconciliar bishop?

The Priestly *Aggiornamento*

Within the reform movements which jolted the Church, the young Latin American clergy had not made the question of celibacy, in general terms, a cause of belligerent non-conformity nor motive for canonical polemics with the hierarchy. This statement does not mean that defections have been few or of little importance in recent years, but without doubt the great majority have not originated from this limitation imposed on the priestly ministry.

On April 20, 1969, the day dedicated throughout the world to Priestly Vocation, Paul VI made an appeal for ways to alleviate the scarcity of clergy in Africa and Latin America. On our continent for some time the total number of priests has been low in relation to the number of parishioners. The deficit has been aggravated in recent years by the decreasing number of aspirants to the ecclesiastical ministry, and by the fact that more and more priests, including bishops, have been hanging up their soutanes because of disillusionment or because of the appeal of marriage.

Before this phenomenon of desertion reached the present massive proportions, the Vatican became concerned, and with good cause. With a great majority of Catholics among its 258,461,490 inhabitants Latin America could count only 43,814 priests, while the United States with a Catholic minority among its 211,700,000 people has 58,865 priests.

Not a day passed without some press account of a priest's leaving the ministry to be married by Catholic rites while reaffirming his profession of the faith. The tendency among Latin American clergy has been to follow the line of their European and United States colleagues although until now that inclination seemed limited. Each case is viewed as a personal problem rather than a canonical problem. News stories have continued to create excitement; for example, the story from Philadelphia concerning the marriage of Father George C. Hafner to his secretary performed officially in Temple University by Paul Mayer, another married priest.

Logically, is it possible to attribute priestly desertion exclusively to clerical celibacy, as some allege? In spite of the weight of publicity accorded to the resignations of United States clergy, the indices in Latin America are noticeably higher in comparison to those in the United States and Canada. In this part of the hemisphere 3.02 percent have left their sacred calling, but in Anglo-Saxon America including Canada, only .98 percent have left. The comparison is significant—in North America, less than one in every hundred; in Latin America, more than three. What is the explanation for the many priestly desertions in Latin America?

In a spirit of recovering for the Church its primitive standing, with wisdom and sincerity the young priests have given a high place among their concerns to the theory and practice of genuine Christianity as they understand it; that is, the redemption of the humble and the oppressed. Contact with them, with their misery and their customs, implies an adventure which is dangerous for the Old Church. The unhappy fate of Cardinal Suhard's experience with worker-priests aroused a grave fear that when priests faced the ideological struggle with Marxists in factories and unions, their concern about work and temporal organization would interfere with their proper activities. The same concern could prompt priests to withdraw from the field of education. It is certain that exposure to the irrational and brutal exploitation of workers and peasants led post-conciliar priests to study plans and formulas concerning equity in the production of consumer goods and justice in the labor system and distribution of wealth.

The rank-and-file priests of Latin America soon became conscious of the dramas of their people brought to view by John XXIII, *Populorum Progressio,* Vatican Council II, and the final document issued by the Latin American Episcopal Conference convened in Medellín in 1968. Days passed; months passed. The

Young Church came to believe that anything constructive would just remain on paper. They were depressed by a sense of frustration in the face of increasingly acute social problems ignored by a hierarchy decorated with honors and medals by the oligarchies. None of those causes for anguish troubled the consciences of United States and Canadian priests who carried on their ministries in affluent societies.

The Latin American Episcopal Conference which met in Argentina recognized that source of hopelessness. It stated that "The incoherence in the commitments reached at Medellín and their inadequate realization on both the national and diocesan levels create tension and frustration among many groups of priests. Even more serious are the instances when the means for dialogue and co-responsibility between bishops and priests, sponsored by the Council at Medellín, do not function properly."

As the Old Church changed its attitude, flattery and pressure from military and oligarchic governments diminished.

The conformist hierarchy shunned all contact with workers, peasants, and the poor. They labeled anyone communist who asked them to descend from their thrones, or, if the mercy of their cold charity softened them, labeled them a mere rebel without condemnatory epithets. Very few Latin American prelates shared the views of the Brazilian Bishop Mota, set forth in *Le Monde* of Paris in October, 1964. On the eve of the Council he wrote, "If we do not send some priests especially prepared to live and work with laborers and with the poor, then, we, the bishops, will fail to understand them since we do not live in contact with them."

The hierarchy's remoteness from reality and its contempt for the vital drama of the lives of the majority led to grave deteriorations in the *presbyterium,* a significant relationship in the beginning of the Church when the bishop lived surrounded by his clergy, listened to them, and loved them. Those mini-pontiffs, Bolatti in Argentina and Uribe Urdaneta in Colombia, typified the most evident and clamorous distortions of the pastoral mission among Latin American clergy. A certain mood of disappointment aggravated by the prelates' lack of sensitivity spread among the clergy in the countryside and in the slums. Then began the desertions of those convinced that they could not fulfil the positive social function of the ministry.

Celibacy was a secondary problem. Ancestral prejudices, which was the essence of the faith for believers living in the underdeveloped countries, blocked the way out of the alley. For them, celibacy is an essential part of the priest-magic, a magic aura given by the divine power which surrounds that being who is worthy of adoration for his capacity to exorcise malign spirits. He is a being superior to other mortals because he publicly renounces sexual gratification in a primitive society in which the only earthly felicities are pleasures of the flesh, a consequence of original sin and the cause of the population explosion.

It did not matter that the priest committed a sin, one essentially provisional. Clandestine violation of the prohibition is accepted, propitiated, praised. The important thing is for the priest not to contract a marriage, a sacrament which ties indissoluble bonds. Thus the number of illegitimate children increases. A defrocked priest cannot perform any service to the Latin American Church, not because it violates Canon Law, but because it is a scandalous matter; by entering a marriage contract he has ceased being different from other men. That ingenuous belief was born of the pre-logical mental habit of assigning all effects to supernatural causes. The efficacy of the sorcerer, of the priest-magician, depended on what distinguished him from the supplicant—on his esoteric differentiation from the masses. This was the understanding of the Old Church. St. Matthew explained celibacy and exalted it (Matt. 19:12, King James Version): "For there are some eunuchs, which were so born from their mother's womb: and there are some eunuchs, which were made eunuchs of men: and there be eunuchs, which have made themselves eunuchs for the kingdom of heaven's sake."

Ecclesiastical celibacy is relatively new in the Church, having become a practice in the High Middle Ages. It was unknown in the primitive Church. Efforts to establish it among the apostles lack historical exactness. Those fishermen, preachers, and martyrs who accompanied Jesus in Galilee even to Calvary were married men. In the second century, Clement of Alexandria, a Church Father, sustained the position that none of them was a bachelor. William E. Phipps, a professor and researcher in the United States, recently emphasized the point, noting that "When they asked for his point of view on the question, Christ reaffirmed the Genesis ideal in which man and woman were created for each other. The years between the infancy and public life of Jesus, about which the Gospels are silent, cover the period in Hebrew society when one was expected to become engaged and married."

Father Salvador Ortiz, parish priest of Ciudad Satélite in Mexico City, expressed the opinion that "celibacy occurs as a custom, as an adornment of the priesthood. But it would not be a sin if competent authorities were to remove the restriction, for Christ did not ask his priests to be celibate."

In the first heroic centuries of the Church, celibacy was not obligatory for ministers, not even for the highest ecclesiastic dignitaries. Today the Holy See accepts the tradition for the Marionite and Armenian clergy, wholly dependent on Roman Catholicism. St. Peter, one of the major authorities of the Church, constrained to give counsel of moderation to his bishops, wrote (I Tim. 3: 1–3, King James Version): "If a man desire the office of bishop, he desireth a good work. A bishop must then be blameless, the husband of one wife, vigilant, sober, of good behavior, given to hospitality, apt to teach; not given to wine, no striker, not greedy of filthy lucre, but patient, not a brawler, not covetous." St. Cyril of Jerusalem limited himself simply to recommending celibacy. When a law of A.D. 300 required the priesthood to abstain from any carnal knowledge of their wives, the women received merciful treatment from Pope Honorio who said, "These women who by their manner of living have made their husbands worthy of the priesthood ought not to be abandoned on account of love for chastity."

Since 1123 when Pope Calixtus II in the Lateran Council finally prohibited marriage of priests, the Church has had a difficult problem. In view of the actual situation of the priesthood in Latin America, some ask themselves when the universal movement against celibacy will lead to a crisis, with the deaconate being the only solution available. In Paul VI's name the encyclical *Sacerdotalis Celibatus* of June 24, 1967 shut off any other solution.

After the Pope's encyclical ratifying the institution of celibacy, the procession of priests in Latin America who chose married life continued despite the dilemma put before them in such absolute terms. The most publicized case of a defrocked priest in Latin America, comparable only to that of Monsignor Giovanni Musante of the Vatican court, was that of the Auxiliary Bishop of Lima, Mario Renato Cornejo Ravadero. Bishop Cornejo Ravadero had become one of the most prestigious among the Peruvian prelates, and had represented the hierarchy at the Latin American Episcopal Conference. The forty-one-year-old bishop disappeared without notice in February, 1969, and in March resigned from his ecclesiastic functions. In order to quiet rumors the Archbishop issued a communication in which he attributed the desertion to a crisis in faith, and denied rumors of a civil marriage of the Bishop in Buenos Aires. In the Argentine capital there was talk about a marriage performed on February 21. Speculation pervaded Catholic sectors of the continent, but the people's curiosity was somewhat deflected by the petroleum dispute between the Peruvian military regime and the White House. The family of the bride revealed the news: Cornejo Ravadero had married Marta Fernández Treviño, previously an agent of the Federal Police of Argentina, in the Buenos Aires registry at Juncal and Carlos Pellegrini Streets on March 10. The emissaries which the Peruvian Cardinal Landázuri Ricketts had sent to Buenos Aires failed to dissuade the Bishop. The following week, Father Luis Casado of the Congregation Paul in Chiclayo hung up his habit and left for Venezuela to take up civil life again.

At the other extreme of motivations and procedures from the Peruvian bishop was the retirement of the Sinologist and Jesuit doctor of social sciences, the Mexican Father Felipe Pardinas Illanes. He explained to the readers of *Novedades* of Mexico City that,

As it is known, I asked the Pope, Paul VI, for full secularization which he conceded to me, and with the subsequent affirmative reply of the Vatican, I was married under both laws (civil and canonical). I decided to present my plea and to submit myself to the process of secularization through irreversible difference of opinion with some procedures of ecclesiastic authority arising some years ago. I continue belonging to the Catholic Church, with the profound certainty that my decision will contribute in the long run to the vitalization of the people of God in Mexico. Thousands of priests throughout the Church have applied for secularization and many have already obtained favorable response to their appeals. Each person's case is peculiar to him, and I do not cite those thousands of brothers as support of my resolution, but as a symptom of a new situation in the Church. For many years I have considered the right of dissent as one of the historic contributions of Christianity to the evolution of the person and of human institutions. I recognize that it is a right exposed to inconstancies, psychological disfunctions, and above all to the immaturity of human beings. I consider, nevertheless, that all these risks are less destructive than a personal and oligarchic authoritarianism. The world's turbulencies are not conducive to giving new dimensions to the concept of human community not only in economic or political terms, but also in religious.

Doctor Felipe Pardinas Illanes presented the nonconformity of the intellectual within an hermetic, impermeable organization. His case is not, of course, a crisis of faith; it is even less a case of happy abandonment of the priestly ministry. He believes, simply, that within the anachronistic structures of a Church grown old, only routine bureaucratic work, which suppresses any initiative in its vertical, absolutist authority, is acceptable.

Paul VI in the Vatican lamented the wave of priestly desertions and offered a very personal explanation. He complained that, "One would say that this generation, filled as it is by the clamor of modern life, is deaf and incapable of hearing the priestly call in its secret and dramatic sense." Figures and percentages supported his words. In relation to the number of inhabitants, the number of priests exercising their ministry is very few in every Latin American country. Each year the number of seminarians is fewer.

The figures in the following table, which appeared in *Excélsior,* Mexico City, August 12, 1970, indicate the crisis of the priesthood in Latin America.

Country	Total population	Number of priests	Number of priests for each 10,000 inhabitants
Argentina	23,706,000	5,216	2.2
Bolivia	3,800,000	798	2.1
Brazil	90,326,000	11,600	1.2
Colombia	19,773,386	5,370	2.7
Costa Rica	1,648,815	331	2.0
Cuba	8,033,000	206	0.2
Chile	8,935,000	2,549	2.8
Ecuador	5,508,000	1,496	2.7
El Salvador	3,151,000	356	1.1
Guatemala	4,717,000	634	1.3
Haiti	4,660,000	452	0.9
Honduras	2,532,000	186	0.7
Mexico	46,482,000	7,354	1.5
Nicaragua	1,783,000	310	1.7
Panama	1,389,489	209	1.5
Paraguay	2,161,000	431	1.9
Peru	13,171,800	2,205	1.6
Dom. Rep.	3,889,000	385	0.9
Uruguay	2,794,000	778	2.7
Venezuela	10,000,000	1,654	1.6

Considering this desolate panorama of the priesthood, Paul VI moans with reason. He blames modern life. In this connection not a few Catholics ask themselves whether the *aggiornamento* (comprising the current setting, the actualization of the Church, the necessity for coming to grips with the changes and exigencies of contemporary life) was not the principal objective of the directions which Vatican Council II set forth. The priesthood and progressive parishioners asked whether the vacillations in the *aggiornamento* might not, consequently, explain the incapacity of youths to hear the calls of a Church with its back to the modern world.

The priestly *aggiornamento* of the Church has been proposed. Sooner or later the Vatican will have no other solution for this priestly crisis than the deaconry such as that proposed through Father Ivan Illich by the Young Church in Cuernavaca. It will be a lay deaconate of married men, based in the home and not the parish, who can live by their trades or professions and administer the sacraments. That will be the ministry of God not of some future society, but of the immediate society, something that the Old Church either cannot understand, or, foolishly or maliciously, attempts to prevent.

6

The Two Synods

In the very heart of the storm provoked by the wisdom of John XXIII to pull Catholicism out of its insane decline, Pope Paul VI used virtuoso diplomacy to battle for reform and to reconcile the contrary currents in the Church.

To carry forward the reforms suggested at Vatican Council II on December 23, 1968 Paul VI convoked an Extraordinary Synod of Bishops to meet in Rome on October 11, 1969. Following the Council, a regulation was established for the General Synod to be considered an assembly of bishops for treating points which "by their nature and importance demand the opinion and prudence of the whole episcopate."

Synods at the diocesan level had performed an invigorating function within the Church, similar to the cooperation experienced in the early Church. In their time the Synods came to be the determining factor in the coresponsibility spontaneously originating from fraternal dialogue and from joint analysis of their own ecclesiastical realities by the bishop, his priests, and the faithful. Forgotten by Canon Law, diocesan synods fell into disuse, asphyxiated by the vertical cult of personality. Each of the ecclesiastical estates was separated from the one below it by the force of an uncommunicative pyramidal edifice until an imposing, triumphal monolith was shaped with the pope alone at its apex, while the nameless masses provided the broad base of supplicants. As in pre-Colombian Teotihuacán of the Toltecs and Kalasasaya of Tiahuanaco, the ceremonial splendor veiled the hopelessness of the downtrodden. In the lives of the forgotten religion is reduced almost to a simple emotional story. It is the opiate of the people, according to the startling flexibility of Karl Marx.

Paul VI issued a *motu propio* on September 15, 1965, creating the Synod which he defined as a means by which cooperation between bishops and the central government of the Church could be intensified as well as their union with the pope. By its very nature it would become a permanent council of bishops of the Universal Church, directly or indirectly subject to the pope who convoked it and presided over it in person or by delegation. Reserved to the Roman pontiff was the right to decide the order of the day and to submit specific questions for examination on which the Synod could report and give counsel under the doctrinal acknowledgment that the pope has supreme power over the Church which he can impart to others when he judges it necessary. That had been in 1965 and four years later still was the thesis which the Roman Curia upheld. Another current—more modern because of its fidelity to forgotten ecclesiastical traditions—supported the thesis that the supreme power over the Universal Church is collegiate and can be exercised in a collegial manner or in person by St. Peter's successor.

These two different interpretations focused the discussion on a fundamental issue: the maintenance in church government of a monarchical absolutism which antedates the French Revolution, or the reorganization of its structures through the acceptance of pluralism and the decentralization of pontifical authority. A second regulation for the Synod issued September 21, 1969 in *Documentation Catholique* began to clarify the point. The regulation established contingent study commissions which would be "little assemblies" integrated by linguistic groups, and it established new rules to make the synodal sessions function better.

An objective of Vatican Council II had been to reestablish communication among the hierarchy, priesthood, and the faithful—among the whole body of the Church. In convoking the Extraordinary Synod of Bishops, Paul VI adopted this objective—with a variation; this synod would be *extraordinary.* Not all the bishops of the world would come to the Vatican, only presidents of episcopal conferences and seventeen prelates selected by the Pope. It would not be a general session in which each episcopal conference had the right to send a delegate for each twenty-five members. Ninety-three presidents of episcopal conferences, or national groups not yet constituted in conferences, would attend. It was observed that possibly those in attendance in this body would have a greater authority, perhaps slightly reflecting the ecclesiastic tendencies of their geographic sectors.

One hundred forty-six high authorites of the Church gathered in Rome. The presidents of episcopal conferences or groups were meticulously catalogued: twenty-nine representatives from Africa, twenty-four from America, twenty-two from Europe, fourteen from Asia, four from Oceania. (The thirteen patriarchs and Oriental metropolitans selected for life were counted among the members. The ecclesiastic assistants of Cardinal Meuchi, Marionite patriarch of Antioch, had the delicacy to travel without their wives.) The Third World, in view of the composition of the Synod, had ceased being the natural ambit of the Catholic Church. As evidence, it may be noted that of the twenty cardinals who directed the Congregations and who were leaders in the Roman Curia, ten were Italians. Superior generals likewise were seated in the Synod, among them the Jesuit Pedro Arrupe and the Abbot Superior of the Benedictine Confederation, Remperto Weakland.

As a final consideration of the Synod's agenda, Paul VI called to Rome the thirty most eminent theologians of Catholicism from eighteen countries, as suggested by the episcopal conferences. They ranged in views from the ultra-conservative Yugoslav, Cardinal Franjo Seper, Provost of the Inquisition, to the erudite German Jesuit, Karl Rahner, and the Swiss theologian, Hans Küng, who were of a decidedly progressive tendency. Although the Synod was obliged to maintain hermetic secrecy, the objectives of the material for its study proved promising; that is, the realization, renovation, and adaptation everywhere of the decrees of the recent Council, and the special examination of the crisis between the authority of the pope and the liberty of theological investigation. The purpose, it seems, was to make way for acknowledging the need for granting greater autonomy to bishops and greater liberty to episcopal conferences to expand their agendas, to go forward with their deliberations, and to arrive at conclusions. What direction should the episcopal conference take in order to be competent in the future to interpret their regional affairs beyond the patterns established by the Roman Curia?

At a Vatican press conference on September 9, the Polish Bishop Ladislas Rubin, named Secretary General of the Synod by Paul VI, dissipated whatever doubt existed about pontifical right to exercise supreme authority in the Church independently of the episcopate. He held that Vatican Council II, on declaring that the pope has universal, full, and supreme power in the Church and that he can always exercise it freely, had indicated the doctrinal point of departure for Catholicism in this respect.

The thirty theologians then arrived in Rome. They would be advisers to the episcopal assembly, "in secret, nor surprisingly," according to an expression in *L'Osservatore Romano.* When His Holiness opened the meeting of the International Theological Commission on October 5, 1969, in the Matilda Chapel of the Vatican, he declared to its members that "all that which restrains or combats the authority and security of Papal Magistery threatens the one true Church." Martin Luther's ghost still haunted the Eternal City. No one in orthodox Catholicism was impugning pontifical rule *ex cathedra.* The point at issue was another matter which the Synod demonstrated and which Paul VI accepted.

The Theological Commission provided the first surprise. At the conclusion of the meeting it made public a communique in favor of pluralism in theological thought; that is, it recognized that conflicting ideas can exist in ecclesiastical doctrine. It was a breakthrough of liberal thought, in open contradiction to the intimidations and repression exercised by the Roman Curia through the Congregation for the Propagation of the Faith. The Synod having run its course, bishops and theologians from three continents convened in the Vatican to discuss in great secrecy with experts in the Roman Curia the liberty—diversity or pluralism—which ought to be conceded to theological meetings. Among those attending were Karl Rahner and Edward Schiellebeek of Holland whose essays the Holy Office had minutely examined for heresy the year before.

The venerable echoes of *Vani Creator Spiritus* with which the Pope and theologians implored for guidance from the Holy Spirit had hardly died away in the Matilda Chapel when Catholicism again demonstrated its vital spirit. Young priests from Europe and America were arriving in Rome determined to obtain a hearing from the Holy See. Joost Reuten of Holland, who presided over the Assembly of European Priests, emphasized their determination to hold a meeting of genuine deeds, not just words. French, Belgian, Dutch, Portuguese, German, Austrian, Italian and Spanish priests together with ecclesiastical observers from the United States and Latin America assembled at the Valdesian College a few yards from the Vatican. They explained that "We have had to meet in a Protestant institution because no Catholic hall was open to us."

Theirs was intelligently directed energy stimulating life and counteracting that which might diminish the faith through trembling reflexes of paralysis or which might lead to disgust. They had in hand a thousand dollars, but the total cost of their meeting was three thousand. The Belgian Father Robert Detry lamented, "Our own communities sent us money, but their funds were inadequate to cover the cost of the meeting." Their meeting was the continuation of the movement which had begun the previous July at Chur, a Swiss town where the European Conference of Bishops had gathered. The Vatican had assumed a hostile attitude toward that meeting, and now observed the assembly at the Valdesian College with the same lack of enthusiasm.

On the former occasion the desire of the progressive clergy to be heard by the European bishops had been repulsed. The Vatican announced that if a similar petition was presented to the Synod it would receive the same fate. On this occasion the revolutionary priests were more daring; they appealed for an audience with the Pope. They celebrated Masses in the poor parishes on the outskirts of Rome, and engaged in polemics with Father Federico Alesandrini, director of the official Vatican weekly, *L'Osservatore Della Dominica.*

The Belgian priests presented a working document which included the following points:

1. For many people the Papacy is a shocking matter; the need for a complete reform in the hierarchical structure of the Church cannot be deferred.

2. The Church must adapt itself to modern life and to man's real needs, and this means that it must become more democratic.
3. Every member of the Church ought to have the liberty to express his ideas, while a full and complete responsibility must be allowed the local churches.
4. Priests must help the poor, but they must never appear as companions of the powerful.

For its part the delegation from Holland in its charges impugned "the manipulations of the Roman Curia"; censorship in general, and in particular that which had been applied to the Bishop of Olinda and Recife, Helder Cámara, who had just been prohibited by that same Curia from speaking outside his diocese; and the financial power of the Church which, in the opinion of the European *contestatarios,* affects the position of the Church in the contemporary world so that it is no longer the defender of the poor and the oppressed. The delegation held that "In Latin America the Church is at the service of the rich and the landowners and dares not break with governments which suppress liberty. Nor has it broken relations with governments which have suppressed liberty in Greece, Portugal, or the Philippines. In the United States the Church has not taken a position against the war in Vietnam, and in South Africa it does not reject the policy of apartheid. As a financial power, the Roman Church is a discredit to the gospel of the poor and is no longer worthy of confidence."

When two hundred priests of that persuasion arrived in Rome on October 7 for the meeting which the Italian press labeled the Shadow-Synod, they sent Paul VI the following message:

Holy Father: In the name of the European assembly of Priests, we respectfully state that we are meeting in Rome, your diocese, from October 10 to 16. The delegates from many European countries and a certain number of observers from the United States will engage in discussions on the theme, *A Liberated Church to Liberate the World.* We assemble in Rome to make a serious and objective contribution to the great dialogue opened in the bosom of the Church by the Council and by your obligation with respect to liberty, progress, and justice, an obligation what you yourself have assumed in your encyclical *Populorum Progressio* and in your appeal from Geneva. We know that the Episcopal Synod, meeting under your presidency, will be very important. We pray that it may deliberate in peace and with the respect due the Eternal City, but we hope it will show clearly to men of today that the Church, image of Christ, wants to remain increasingly a servant of the faithful, the poor, and the free. We implore earnestly that Your Holiness will condescend to bless our work and accept the testimony of our filial affection.

Paul VI named as presiding officers of the Extraordinary Synod of Bishops three cardinals who had no clearly defined position in the two currents of thought apparent in the meeting: Carlo Confalonieri, an Italian who was secretary of the Consistorial Congregation; Angelo Rossi, Brazilian Bishop of São Paulo; and Valerian Gracias, Pakistani Bishop of Bombay.

Expectation began to center on the statements of four European cardinals who were enthusiastic fighters for transcendental reforms within the Church, especially with regard to the adoption of pluralism, collegiality, and coresponsibility. They were Leo Joseph Suenens, Archbishop of Brussels; the German Julius Doepfner, Archbishop of Munich and Freising; Bernard Alfrink of Holland, Archbishop of Utrecht; and the Austrian Franziskus König, Archbishop of Vienna. Suenens is the author of the celebrated essay, *Church, what do you have to say for yourself?*, who had raised the problem of the schema *Ecclesia* at the end of the first session of Vatican II; he is an advocate of episcopal collegiality, and an advocate of new and modern stimuli to the responsibility of the laity in the diocese, of the reorganization of the Roman Curia, of the revision of the role of nuncios, and of reforms in the Canon Law for the purpose of achieving collegiality. The last three were all non-conformists with respect to the encyclical *Humanae Vitae*.

The working papers and the conclusions of the Shadow-Synod promoted the health of the Church, sick with the disease of perfection. Its agenda included such matters as the association of the laity and clergy in the election of bishops instead of the selection in reality by the pope, and the election of the Supreme Pontiff by the Synod of Bishops instead of by the College of Cardinals.

This had become an insoluble matter in the reform of the Church's structure. On September 23, 1969 Salvatore Baldassari, Bishop of Ravenna and a typical member of the Italian hierarchy, proposed in the Catholic review of Bologna, *Il Regno,* that it was the bishops, not the cardinals, who elected the pope. He stated, "The pope is elected by a college of a very respectable ecclesiastical nature and one which indubitably has many merits. But around the pope, with the pope, and under the pope is a college of divine origin: the Episcopal College." The major objection to the proposal, according to the Ravenna prelate, would be that the cardinals represent electors almost kin to the pope; that is, the Roman clergy and the Roman people. But for Bishop Baldassari the objection was simply a figment of the imagination.

Likewise, the Shadow-Synod proposed a limitation on periods of service, which would be renewable, for the pope and the bishops, cancelling the present practice of life tenure; the establishment of the right of the Synod of Bishops to decide its own agenda and meeting dates instead of the pope's exercising those rights, thus putting life into a principle which Vatican Council II had defined; the suppression of "priestly caste" which the Italian clergy characterized as "privileged and powerful oligarchy"; authorization for priests to earn their living in secular occupations, even in politics and labor unions, without giving up their ministry; and "cancellation of the Roman pontifical absolutism, because it is considered, also, the principal obstacle to the restoration of Christian unity among Catholic, Anglican, and Protestant groups."

In matters concerning the "separated brothers," Vatican overtures had not been particularly persistent; nor had the intimations of friendly intercourse with Marxists and atheists to whom John XXIII had offered his paternal hand. Now, suddenly, Cardinal Alfredo Ottaviani declared still in effect the excommunication decreed by the Holy Office in July, 1949 against communists and those who participated in their struggles and doctrines. The wicked malice of some critics led them to conclude that the excommunication was pronounced on the eve of some Italian elections in which the fate of the government of Alcide de Gasperi was at stake in order to help the Christian Democrats gain favor.

Antagonized by extreme right terrorists, offended by the sectarian voices of the Old Church, just before beginning their deliberations the members of the Shadow-Synod received a word of encouragement. The German theologian Karl Rahner, named by Paul VI to the International Theological Commission, told them publicly, "Do not be disturbed if they call you schismatics or communists. While you preach God's message with faith and sincerity, you are safe." Safe before God. Less so before men. They were attacked in St. Peter's Square, under the pontifical balcony itself, on Sunday morning, October 12, two days after they had begun their deliberations. For their own benefit the extremists had put the forces of attack into action. Among them were the *Deutscher Bund Gott mit Uns* of West Germany, the *Guerillas de Cristo Rey* of Spain, and the *Unión Católica Lusitana* of Portugal. The following day Vatican Radio condemned their aggression as "vain efforts of a group of pretended crusaders for the Council, the meaning and purposes of which they do not understand."

Through intermediaries Paul VI promised the Shadow-Synod to give attention to its conclusions. Also, bishops of Germany, Austria, Spain, France, and Holland who were members of the Extraordinary Synod received their compatriots in the Assembly of European Priests in special audiences. Cardinal Alfrink of Holland foresaw that, "If we, the bishops, do not support the priests' requests, we run the risk that they will proceed without us to try to purify and renew the Church, and this would be conducive to greater confusion among the faithful."

At the inauguration of the Episcopal Synod, Paul VI carefully confirmed pontifical authority and made a slight, illusory opening to collegiality. He said, "The government of the Church should not take on the appearances and norms of secular regimes, which today are guided by democratic institutions which are sometimes irresponsible and given to excesses, nor of totalitarian forms which are contrary to man's dignity."

At the same time he weakened the possibilities of pluralism by indicating that it is antithetical to ecumenical conformity, saying, "The common welfare of the Church should not be compromised by special autonomies and excessive disparities which might prejudice that unity and charity which is essential in making the Church one heart and one soul, and which might favor rivalries and bruised egos."

Pope Paul's concepts were understood as the required orientation for the Synod. Many authorized voices within and without the Synod wondered, with greater or lesser stridency and with haste, why Paul VI had called the assembly if he, as the highest authority in the Church, had already untied the two knots which were, at least theoretically, what selected bishops and cardinals had been called to Rome to consider. Doubt developed that the meeting would be able to follow through with the openings to the world of today which Vatican Council II had initiated.

Prematurely, in turn, observers considered that the Old Church had been victorious. With manifest delight those holding back the Church were anticipating a triumph that by no means had been fully attained. At that moment Cardinal Danielou recalled Vatican Council II with strong reproach, saying that if it had borne fruit, it had brought a crisis in the western world with misled priests, weakening of faith among the young and the decline of spiritual life. His conclusion was obvious. In order to face these problems, the Church needed a firm, united authority— that of the pope. Raymond Tchidimbo, since 1968 Archbishop of Spain's African possessions, supported him.

Cardinals Suenens, Alfrink, König and, from France, Marty, insisted upon the urgency of a major consultation between the bishops and the pope. Cardinals Heenan of Great Britain and Doepfner of Germany seconded them. Cardinals Carter of Canada and Conway of North Ireland, scourged by religious disturbances growing out of discrimination against Catholics, shared that view. Carter, the Canadian Primate, explained the basis for his view by saying that no man, whatever his position might be, can be in command of all problems. Consequently, a greater and more intense participation in responsibilities by the pope and his bishops is more necessary than ever.

Cardinal Carter and fourteen United States theologians made a plea to Rome to renounce its centralization of power. They bore in mind the dissentions provoked by the encyclical *Humanae Vitae.* Cardinal François Marty, Archbishop of Paris, also expressed the point without any ambiguity, adding, "I believe that all the prelates think that they ought to do everything possible to prevent a repetition." The Synod recommended that the pope and bishops refrain from making declarations or taking important decisions without previous mutual consultations concerning the consequences to all aspects of the Church.

Pedro Arrupe, General of the Jesuits, clarified Synodal thought by saying, "The fact that the pope does not exercise his authority in isolation but in personal contact and with recognition of actual difficulties will do much to help correct the image that public opinion has formed of the pope."

The Synod achieved full agreement. With studied sluggishness, it continued changes admitted by Vatican Council II. The Church did not cancel its intention of taking a place in the world in which we live. If the *aggiornamento* ("magic word which had pushed many far beyond what is fitting," in Paul VI's moderating phrase) did not receive stimuli from the Synod in accord with the chimeras which the most progressive sectors of the Church had formed, neither was it the backward step which the reactionary elements desired.

Bishop Carter described the Synod as a surgical operation which will improve the circulation of Christ's Blood. Cardinal Suenens, equally graphic, compared it to an elevator which stops on the third floor but was expected on the tenth. Looked at from below, it seems high; but viewed from above, it seems very low. What was certain was that the Synod continued the reform process of Vatican Council II, which Schiellebeek of Holland defined as a decentralization upwards: "Rome will decentralize itself in order to center itself on Christ."

In regard to the question of collegiality or the absolutism of pontifical authority, the Synod welcomed eclectic formulas in its proposals on democratization as an alternative to centralism. It asked for participation by the bishops in Church decisions, and for clarification of the bishops' local authority. With regard to pluralism as an antinomy to colonialism, which related to the question of autonomy of the national Churches to study problems in their respective zones or their subordination to the Roman Curia, the Synod favored a greater degree of liberty which looked to future synods to solicit greater participation from the bishops in the preparation of agendas with a view to improving collegiate government.

The Synod found a subtle formula for defining papal authority, leaving St. Peter's successor to exercise his prudence. Instead of the disjunction *primate or collegiality,* it suggested *primate and collegiality*—a collegiality which would not destroy the primate, and a primacy which would be exercised within collegiality. The need for recognizing a certain liberty for national Churches and their regional organization, the episcopal conference, had been indicated on account of the Latin American case of CELAM, whose proposals for dealing with the realities of the region had been rather exact up to that time. From the above recommendations were derived those related to the internationalization of the Roman Curia to make it responsive to the world episcopate: the need of a greater fidelity to the pope's thought, and greater respect for decisions of episcopal conferences by nuncios and apostolic delegates; and, the request for a beginning of collegiality in the election of the pope as well as in other matters. To achieve a more direct relation between the pope and the bishops, it was held advisable that the Episcopal Conference should meet every two years by its own right, and not just on an occasional call by the Holy See. Its agenda should not be established by the Roman Curia but should be open to the suggestions of the episcopal conferences. The Roman Curia, likewise, should advance the cases of clergy who have hung up their soutanes and cases of marriage annulments.

Examination of the question of family planning was deferred until the next Episcopal Synod, in anticipation of a study by an advisory commission of expert theologians and canonists. According to a proposal by François Marty, Archbishop of Paris, that same assembly of bishops should examine the matter of the priesthood in general and of celibacy in particular. At the conclusion of the Synod after eighteen days of sessions in the Basilica of

Santa María la Mayor, Paul VI, on October 25, 1969, the day after his seventy-second birthday, recognized celibacy as "a super-human virtue which requires supernatural support."

The young Latin American clergy will have the possibility of carrying on the *aggiornamento* to the degree that Paul VI accepted the Synod's recommendations. A second condition will be that it encounter no hostility and be understood by the regional authorities of the Old Church.

The Synod had started from the conviction, not entirely correct, that all the obstacles the *aggiornamento* had encountered came from the Roman Curia. That may have been true for Europe. In Latin America the conformist hierarchy was customarily the most recalcitrant element toward the Church's new social endeavors. The progressive clergy of our area had the task of bringing about collegiality and co-responsibility on the diocesan level which had germinated at pontifical heights. It is going to be an arduous and risky effort in many Latin American archdioceses. Violence in many forms will prevent modernization of the Church. Intermingled with the pre-conciliar hierarchies, the untouchables will be even stronger in their entrenched privileges. The Synod's conclusions will make no impression on them. In defense of anachronistic privilege, they will try to smother the least discrepancy with the ancient concept and exercise of episcopal authority, seldom used to evaluate the economic and political problems which occasion the violence of the powerful.

That which has been observed among the French priests, without incurring heresy, is certain for priests in Latin America. The President of the French Episcopal Conference, Monsignor Guyot, said in the Council, on studying the plan of the "Pastoral Function of Bishops," that,

What many priests actually desire in their relations with their bishops is the development of a climate of mutual confidence. They aspire to be able to express frankly their hopes and difficulties, to share their experiences, to propose when possible concrete solutions, and to take certain initiatives. Said in another way, our priests do not want to be charged only with the execution of decisions *from on high,* but desire to participate in developments from the pastoral to the diocesan level so that there can be a true continual collaboration. A similar action agreed upon within the heart of the *presbyterium* assumes that there is at every diocesan level some permanent structure for dialogue in which the bishop is directly or indirectly present. The dialogue in question is that related properly to pastoral matters concerning the well-being of the diocese. It is not reduced to individual and occasional contact between a bishop and his priests, but is dialogue which develops in the whole group (teamwork). In a changing society involving human relations to the degree that ours does, a lack of real, permanent structures means that no pastoral dialogue occurs ... or rather it is a dialogue between deaf persons. With great mutual generosity, a bishop and his priests incur the danger of traveling parallel ways which, it is well known, meet only in infinity. From the pastoral point of view, that is rather late! On the other hand, when a true dialogue and a true collaboration among the diverse apostolic sectors are established, misunderstandings vanish little by little, common thought about essential points of evangelization and the Kingdom of God are set in motion.

In that same Council, Monsignor Jenny, Auxiliary Bishop of Cambrai, said that "the *presbyterium* united with the bishop constitutes 'the bishop' in his fullness."

The theologians of the Young Latin American Church were concerned with the determination of the justice of the popular counter-violence and its scope, limitations, and methods. That was part of their new obligations under theological and ecclesiastic pluralism in accordance with the synodical orientations. After accepting Fidel Castro's observation that "it is not actually the revolutionary struggle that takes the most lives; misery and exploitation are greater destroyers," René Coste, a French professor wrote in *Nouvelle Revue Théologique* in January, 1969 that the encyclical *Populorum Progressio* admitted the legitimacy of revolutionary insurrection in the "case where there is evident and prolonged tyranny which poses great danger to fundamental individual human rights and to the country's well-being. *Evident and prolonged tyranny* is not the only problem producing loss of political rights. According to Professor Coste, "To the degree that man sees his socio-economic rights trampled underfoot, he is the victim of a violence which impedes the development of his personality and can even bring about his death by the slow fire of misery's continuous erosion." This sort of violence is exercised with absolute freedom in Latin America, even in regimes that boast of the respect which they dispense for formal, superficial liberties, which are distractions from the drama underneath.

Left and Right in Relation to the Young Church

Reform of the internal structures of the Latin American Church in relation to the world around it, a cause taken up by the cultivated rank and file clergy and in a few cases by episcopal dignitaries, is forcing new ideological and political definitions. In a few cases the reform movement has begun to breach the timeworn barricades which have been conventionally labeled the "left" and the "right."

The "left," a generally used but oversimplified label, perceives its objectives for the recovery of the exploited classes to be in accord with the post-conciliar orientation followed by the youthful sector of the clergy which, consequently, came to be called "progressive." The common approach to the causes of social injustice encouraged them to develop mutual sympathy. Their shared views united them in the struggle in city streets and in the countryside against the old, backward, dominant, and avaricious castes. Neither group was indifferent to the fact that the establishment continued to consider itself immutable in its negativeness. They realized that no order, no value, however consecrated or sacred those in power might wish to make it appear, could gloss over the exploitation of the masses.

Both groups rebelled against the idealist lie, a mystification which pretends to mitigate or do away with the brutal pressure of reality. They had renounced the ethereal, the evolution of existence through affectations. Their estimation of human life was no longer esthetic or magical. They shared a new humanism which was not concentrated on man only, because "what is human is given to men in the form of things." Misery, they reflected, contributed to the dehumanization of man and all which surrounds him. They rejected the narcissism of the ivory tower and the church, and disdained the intellectual or the politician devoted to selling illusions in the electoral circus. They would not allow themselves to be seduced by the paternalism of the opportunists nor by the pseudo-realism of the technocrats of affluence.

Their mutual attraction was reflexive, a product also of the inequality of the antagonistic forces. The emotion which the struggle engendered reconciled them to its purposes. The weakness of each before the powerful led them to the same conclusion: united they could make a better fight for the cause they supported. That was exactly what the masters and the privileged who continued to control the decrepit economic, social, and political structures feared.

In Argentina and Brazil forward-looking unions and progressive clergy concurred in their objectives and began to harmonize their methods.

No leftist could impugn the final document issued by CELAM (The Latin American Episcopal Conference). Convoked in 1968 in Medellín, provincial capital of one of the most traditional and humanly vigorous socio-economic areas in Latin America, that conference developed the principles of *Progressio Populorum* and Vatican Council II in continental terms. It summarized in a general way, indicating social injustices and economic and political solutions, the thesis which for years, with limited political success, had been shaping Latin American leftist thought. The attitude of CELAM toward all "men of good will" opened the doors of the Church to make way for shared activities on a common ground. Though the Latin American Church proclaimed itself peaceful with respect to a strategy of emancipation, it recognized that situations of extreme injustice authorized self-defense by violence, legitimated, moreover, by the "tacit violence" of an unjust economic and social system.

In order to frustrate any agreement between the progressive clergy and the left, the former were accused of leaning toward communism. The exclusive guardians of authentic Christian doctrine—authenticity to which they, the just, the elect of God, attested—were not unaware of the fact that the priests of the slums and sidewalks with a strong ascendancy among the workers and the poor, by attracting the dispersed left to their following would undermine the foundations of the old order where the declining power of the ruling classes rested. Implacable and arrogant, they turned to their own advantage the actual relation of forces to maintain their benefits from the existing injustice in landholding, in the systems of industrial labor, and in the liberal—for them—distribution of profits and wealth.

Will it be possible for the Young Church and the left to form a united front in Latin America? In France efforts of that nature have broken down, and in Italy appear to have become utopian. In Latin America it is barely possible that the affluent minority will succeed in preventing it through more force or through effective use of their widespread resources, legitimate and illegitimate. It is apparent that the difficulty arises from internal dissentions of the left. Internal disagreements concerning Latin American political strategy have become so intense that they have culminated in doctrinnaire differences. The extreme left in Latin America has been alienated by the conflict between Moscow and Peking. The two factions of the left pour their energies into reciprocal hatred of those two poles of political attraction. Each promotes dogmas for the full administration of its own interests. Those on the left— intellectuals, students, workers, peasants—who in this hemisphere do not militantly support either of those countries on opposite banks of the Ussuri River in Asia, are, however, combatants with the same animosity toward the antagonistic masters of the current Marxist orthodoxy. Sectarianism leads them with equal blindness to ignore the real resistance present in Latin America. The strict discipline in following a given line which each side judges infallible makes them forget, in submission to the provisional present, the transcendent task. In such a moment they begin to recreate fascist tactics. Dogmatic blindness prevents them from taking advantage of actual possibilities.

Surely the democratic left, pleased that the progressive clergy, having accepted their thesis that change is urgent, desires and seeks association with them. It is incumbent upon the left to enrich its views of the surrounding world, to deepen its revolutionary conceptions within the scope of each national framework. But perhaps the achievement of that accord of absolute loyalty to the common purpose within the limits of the struggle is unlikely. The left's concern with getting elected independently of Moscow and Peking continues to be its chief problem. At times it seems almost insuperable since almost all its leaders have made their election to associated bodies a unique mode of personal life.

Paradoxically, the actual dispersion of the Latin American left, its infantile atomization through sectarianism and opportunism, and the fury of its domestic disputes, benefit the Young Church. The disenchantment and frustration of many intellectual and popular nuclei of the left could turn them to the post-conciliar clergy for leadership or for a more congenial, more effective association worthy of greater confidence on account of the clergy's disinterest and social honesty.

The results of Latin American cultural underdevelopment, a natural consequence of economic underdevelopment, are usually felt with greater frustrating force by the left than by any other sector of Latin American thought and political action. The sole exception is Chile.

The question of armed struggle as the proper revolutionary method confuses and divides the Young Church just as it does the left. Both hold the view that the law, converted into a protective armor for the oppressor's privileges, has ceased to be respectable. They agree that it is the privilege of the affluent to resort to that fraudulent legality to justify their tacit violence. On the other hand, they do not reject the conclusion that the new slaves have no other recourse than resort to illegality. They are together up to this point.

They split on the interpretation of the practice of the illegality. Heated arguments arose over whether illegality leads necessarily to physical violence, to daring action; or whether it is positive or negative to permit the oppressors to make use of the total coercive force at their disposal against the oppressed, and make it appear as counter-violence in defense of the only order possible, desirable, or patriotic, with the understanding that "mother country" is one of the most refined and efficient forms of hypocrisy of the ruling class.

Taking into account circumstances in Latin America and in a world solidified into blocs which permitted the United States to enter Santo Domingo and the Soviet Union to invade Czechoslovakia, the only viable tactic up to now has seemed to be passive resistance to oppression like that which allowed a Mahatma Gandhi to confront British colonial power and a Martin Luther King to struggle for the civil rights of blacks against the crushing racist apparatus of the United States.

That was exactly the kind of movement Bishop Helder Cámara wanted to organize on a continental scope, beginning October 12, 1969. The proposal was planned to serve as a sort of cohesive factor among all the Latin American progressive forces with an exceptional leader in Recife. But Rome would allow nothing of the sort. The Bishop disciplined his heart and his capabilities. He remained silent.

Helder Cámara could have relied on battle-tested and veteran allies. On returning to Latin America from Europe, Pedro Arrupe imparted precise instructions to the Jesuits. In the Madrid review, *Índice* on October 5, 1969 he wrote, "For example, the members of the Society of Jesus cannot remain passive in the face of a racist policy. If we do not commit ourselves in cases such as this, or in others such as *institutionalized violence*, we fail in our vocation."

With similar intensity, the "right" began to feel the effects of the post-conciliar attitude of the Young Church. Ever since shortly after Christopher Columbus' arrival on the continent, the economically strong have held the idea that the Church is a natural part of their system of domination. The Church continued to be branded with that imprint, enjoying its consequences. For a period of four centuries, voices within the Church favoring the humble were always considered isolated impertinences, unfortunate heterodoxies, apostasies, or the delirium of perturbed minds. And they were silenced. Discouraged.

That traditional image of the Church at the side and service of the peninsular proprietors, masters of the *encomiendas*, mine owners, traffickers in slaves during the colonial era, and then in the republican period united with their heirs, has encountered in John XXIII's teachings the first bold, profound attempt at radical rectification. The Young Church is struggling against that heritage of the Church, pillar of the colonial system, which its hierarchy had prolonged into the republican period. The Old Church in recent years provided Latin American feudalism the satisfaction of inspiring the Franco clergy during the Spanish Civil War, and of making the cause of fascism its own.

Rome leaned toward the Old Church by filling the highest offices in the Latin American Church according to the social origin of the candidates. As a rule, they came from among the great landowners, the conservative ruling class, the paternalistic masters. Such groups, as a counterstroke, agreed to the evident power of the Church. Contradictions began when the lower classes stopped considering the priesthood as a means of climbing the social ladder, and when cultivated priests, influenced by European Catholic thought, the new encyclicals, and Vatican Council II, became conscious of the fallacies of their ties with the bourgeoisie, whose economic philosophy of liberal origin induced them to legitimatize the oppression of industrial and agricultural production in their countries. The nobility, and within it, its colonial representatives, had fought for their privileges; nothing else mattered. But how should the clergy deal with the bourgeoisie, with the rich heirs of the liberals, persistent in sanctifying their monopolies?

The rich, proxies for the Church, resisted. They were not going to allow themselves to be dislodged from the niches where good conscience was sold to them and their outrages blessed. They had always understood that the Lord, the Virgin, and the saints were the advocates of their harvests, their cattle, and their speculations on the stock market. The progressive clergy tried to weaken those relationships and abandoned their ties with the rich to play, irresponsibly, with the fire of the "worker threat." If we agree that a characteristic of the bourgeoisie is a "little fear of the twentieth century," we must agree that in Latin America it has become an open panic. There is nothing so pitiful as the powerful who are afraid.

The rightist intellectuals, accustomed to the sinecures and calculated exaltations of vanity, fought also to retain their place in the establishment. The plan they had in mind perplexed them, however. They had to answer the question of how communism, understood as a change in structure, should be opposed. They replied, without breaking the vicious circle of their speculations, "with the affirmation of Christian and human values which represent western civilization." How should they define the threatened values? Attempts to formulate definitions put them on the side of those who were rebelling, not against those values, but against the interpretation that the landowners and the manipulators of colonialist finances customarily made for their exclusive benefit.

The progressive clergy were able to continue their heretical fantasies, swelling the communist ranks. Within a few years the record will show that it was merely a transitory inconvenience. The Latin American castes still have two good and loyal allies — the Old Church and Washington. Their understanding with the highest ecclesiastical authorities of the conformist Church confirms them in their conviction that they are the righteous ones. In any emergency their direct lines to Washington guarantee the almost instantaneous presence in the proper place of the Green Berets. While they can rely on the Roman monsignors and the White House, they can sleep comfortably, positive that violent change will be rapidly suppressed and the triumphant will be blessed.

Given that alignment among the potentates, the Young Church found enthusiastic support among the people and the students. Within unions and Catholic centers of higher education their reformist ideas began to force the need for the former to change tactics and for the latter to make thorough revisions. Reforms in the orientation and structure of the Catholic University of Chile were the first and eloquent symptoms of the sensitivity that the Young Church could make felt in Latin American intellectual circles.

The progressive clergy have placed the political parties of the right in a dilemma. Either they take the side of the incoherent masses and gain their favor through the emotional appeal of doctrines they have always combatted, or they continue to aggravate their condition as instruments of a senile and unjust order. It is possible to ask whether, outside of Chile, professional politicians of the Latin American right have sufficient courage to attempt such a liberation. At least, within the current continental panorama, it is doubtful that professional politicians of the right will exchange the apparent stability from which they benefit for the risks of popular struggle. For them the real factors of power continue to be economic monopolies, the Old Church, and the military. That calculation, based on the historical perspective of the continent, has contributed to creating the vacuum that the popular leadership of the progressive, post-conciliar priesthood is filling.

The writings and combativeness of the bishops who supported the victorious elements in the Spanish Civil War aroused fanaticism in the Latin American hierarchy and clergy. In the face of astonishment and protest by the Catholic intelligencia in France, Belgium, Holland, and Italy, a joint pastoral letter from the Spanish prelates—after the fall of País Vasco, governed by a Catholic majority—justified that insurrection. The document characterized the conflict as an "armed plebicite" against the probability of a "communist revolution," concluding with a criticism of the resistance of the Basque clergy. Isidro Gomá y Tomás, Archbishop of Toledo, Cardinal Primate of Spain, named pontifical delegate to the *Junta de Defensa* of Burgos by Pius XI, stated in his proclamations that the traditional Latin American right would again defend the utilization of the advantages which power affords. The pseudo-aristocratic landed proprietors then assumed as their own the incendiary explications of E. Pla y Daniel, Bishop of Salamanca. They overlooked the fact that the collective pastoral letter said that "The war has not been fought to erect an autocratic State over a humiliated people."

Thirty years later the young Spanish clergy was confronting tyranny in the Spanish streets. In Latin America, in Chile as well as in Peru, they cooperated with the Young Church. They protested, resisted, and served time in Spanish jails. Dom Cassiá María Just, Abbot of the famous Montserrat Monastery in Barcelona, exemplified all three forms of confrontation. Once again he became engaged in the fight for freedom of thought and the defense of the Spanish working class. Dom Cassiá María Just had stated in the German periodical *Politik* that

the present political regime has its origin in the bloody victory at the end of the war which divided our country, which continues to be divided between the victors and the defeated in spite of the peace propaganda which the government issues. Since that victory the people who make up the existing Spanish State have seen their right of free speech and association, their right to political and union representation, their right to strike, and the right of ethnic minorities to normal development suppressed in spite of juridical fictions of the *referendum* and the courts which are used to confuse international opinion. We have an example of that in our Monastery. Censorship, actually, has suppressed or mutilated papal and episcopal documents, always ones that deal with personal human rights; and today's press has distorted the summaries of the positions of the few bishops who have manifested their non-conformity to the repressive measures taken by the government. . . .

The principal obligation of the Church is to proclaim the Gospel to its ultimate consequences, to all the orders of human life, individual and social. Perhaps this is its last opportunity before a scandalized people to atone for its feudal subjugation to the Franco regime which has materially protected the Church but has suavely muzzled it for thirty years.

Not a few Spanish priests of the same tendency as the Abbot of Montserrat have been expelled, under accusation of subversion, from Colombia, Argentina, and Paraguay for having organized congregations in the poorest slums of the congested cities. The Old Latin American Church took its quarrel with them to Rome, alleging, with malicious misunderstanding of a task which cannot be limited by boundaries and discriminations, that the Spanish priests "were trying to put into practice what they could not accomplish in their own country." The Latin American Pontifical Commission did not embarrass the rebellious Spanish clergy by reproaching them. The truth is simple; the aged right is beginning to lose its triumphal ally in Spain as well as in this part of the world.

A Catholic Continent

Statistically, Latin America is 99 per cent Catholic. That figure can serve as a starting point for examining some rather complex approximations and conclusions. Is it true that the immense majority of Latin Americans are Catholic, or is it just an often repeated statement that has come to be accepted as so evident that it needs no verification? Recent investigations indicate that only 14 per cent of those called Catholic in Latin America are "practicing Catholics," meaning those who attend Mass on Sundays and feast days, take communion once a year, and have received the sacraments befitting their age and status.

Other data might clarify matters. Latin America has a very high percentage of illegitimate children, even to the point that marriage as a sacrament inspired by St. Paul's letter to the Ephesians has become almost an unknown institution in Latin America, reserved to the minorities of the socially prominent and a few white-collar workers grouped by some analysts under the ambiguous label "middle class." The highest figures for illegitimacy for each 100 inhabitants are: Panama with 69; Guatemala, 67.9; El Salvador, 64.7; the Dominican Republic, 60.5; and Venezuela, 53.7. The lowest are: Brazil, 12.9; Chile, 16.6; Bolivia, 17.2; Colombia, 22.6; and Costa Rica, 23.8. For comparison with countries outside the continent, we may note that Germany has the highest rate with only 12.1, and Japan has the lowest with 1.1.

It is safe to venture the assertion that in Latin America the moral influence of the Church in the basic nucleus of society—the family—is very weak. Universally the Catholic Church has lost ground. Father Pedro Arrupe noted that in 1963 it had included 18 per cent of the world's population but five years later, scarcely 16 per cent.

Some attribute the phenomenon to an insufficient number of priests—a pious interpretation which twists the effect of a problem into a cause. The scarcity of Latin American ecclesiastics indicates the decline of prestige or decrease in spiritual authority of the institution in that area. Explanation for the Church's lack of vigor requires an objective view of the way it presents itself through its highest dignitaries to millions of men, women, and children who lack basic needs, beginning with the most important—good health.

One of the merits the progressive clergy derives from its efforts to change the image of the Church which was engraved on the consciousness of the great majority during the course of four hundred years of history. The Church as an institution has lived luxuriously, unmindful of the fate of the poor in a continent where the rich, who constitute by far the least numerous class, are isolated in pomposity and haughtiness. The Old Church has concentrated only on the aspects of temporal power which landowners, politicians, and the military bestowed upon it in grateful return for favors. Such an intimate association has encouraged it to look with disfavor on any popular movements for change. Its attitude has solidified the widespread anti-clerical passion of workers, peasants, and intellectuals whose opposition, in turn, intensified the proclivity of the hierarchy for the groups who protect them—those most characterized by the power to oppress.

The miserable ones have always visualized the ecclesiastical hierarchy garbed in folds of silk lightly brushing the carpet, with long palliums about their necks, in clouds of incense, presiding over corteges, triumphal or funereal, of the privileged classes. Enchanting pageantry followed at a great distance by immense multitudes without a crumb of bread, temporarily dazzled behind the bayonets. The Jesuit Salvador Freixedo recalled with certainty that,

In South America it is a common idea among ordinary people that the Church—the clergy and, above all, the hierarchy—are intimately allied with the great and the powerful. Unfortunately many actions confirm that view. Seldom do we read in the *Gospel* that Christ talked with the great men of his time. On those few occasions, he was reprimanding them and making fearsome and indisputable accusations against them. Today the hierarchy could do the same. Nevertheless, we see them, with a few glorious exceptions, in the excellent friendly relations which shock the people so much. In the first place, it is an undeniable fact that many bishops appear much more frequently in the houses of the rich than in those of the poor or even the middle class. A further irritation is the fact that the greater part of the clergy and hierarchy come from the humble class but have quickly found the way to the luxurious mansions.

His Puerto Rican diocesan superiors condemned Freixedo in the style of Roman monsignors. The island's Jesuit high command diplomatically facilitated his departure from the Society of Jesus. Freixedo was held guilty of grave offenses against the Church. On October 5, 1969, shortly after his fellow soldier in the Society of Jesus had been ecclesiastically defamed, Father Pedro Arrupe, on arriving in Europe and having analyzed what he had seen, declared in Madrid with jewel-like brevity that perhaps he had failed his distant, wordy, and equally sincere, Puerto Rican disciple, for "Many times we have not completely accomplished our mission for lack of liberty arising from political compromises with the ruling society and with the powerful."

Among the multitudes who "fainted, and were scattered abroad, as sheep having no shepherd" (Matt. 9:36, King James Version), Jesus preached the Sermon on the Mount. Before those poor people, from among whom came the Twelve Apostles, He delivered His discourse on the Kingdom and on following the Father. Those people possessed neither light nor hope, were made hostile by the fratricidal Zealot, were vilified by Roman imperialism, and were put in torment by Herod's designs. Now they are the multitude of *misereor super turbas* (Mark 6:34) whom the Old Church in Latin America wants to ignore. This foolish disdain masks itself by calling itself Christian. The Sermon on the Mount—"Blessed *are* they which do hunger and thirst after righteousness: for they shall be filled" (Matt. 5:6, King James Version)—is doctrine and tradition which cannot be renounced within the categories which

Pope Paul VI set forth with respect to tradition in his address to the cardinals in the Basilica of St. Peter on November 5, 1969. According to the Pope, there are four categories of tradition in the Church: that which cannot be renounced; that which is antecedent but is not necessary in itself; that which is customary but is open to question; and that which is old, superfluous, prejudicial, and as such deserves renunciation and perhaps vigorous reform. The Old Latin American Church has made its bonds with the affluent groups, and in its forgetfulness of poverty and the poor has made a "prejudicial tradition . . . deserving vigorous reform."

The Young Latin American Church seeks to eliminate that tradition. It longs for the Church to fulfill its original purposes. The clergy who propose it are placed in a dilemma of conscience requiring a choice between being faithful to liberation or to the institutional Church, even though CELAM recognized at the meeting in Medellín that "there is a seizure of conscience, an ambience of collective anguish, and exigencies calling for radical change, global, urgent, and audacious in relation to total liberation. As sons of their times and circumstances, many priests are intimately tied to this situation."

What possibilities do the progressive clergy have to achieve that liberation which is supported by recent encyclicals, the conclusions of Vatican Council II, and CELAM? The possibilities seem to have been weighed in Rome. The reticence of the Vatican Curia and the difficulties raised by the Latin American hierarchy minimize and disorient the likelihood of finding solutions. The priests who have adopted reform find themselves facing innumerable obstacles: the open resistance of conformist prelates who delight in the absolutism and glitter that tries to hide injustice; ignorance and fetishism cultivated among the masses for generations by those who monopolize opportunity; the obtuseness of the left enjoying its controversies to the fullest. The Young Church's proposals for social reforms, scientific and canonical, are arrayed against those three bastions of that same protective wall of the medieval castle of anachronistic privileges.

Nevertheless, there are some rays of hope, and the efforts and sacrifices of the ecclesiastic revolutionaries are not sterile. The

Church wants to speak and hear the truth. The inefficacy of the Old Church, its opposition to or its slowness in carrying out conciliar orientations, its image of enchantment with the rich and powerful have already been denounced in spite of the Holy Office. As Father Pedro Arrupe, General of the Society of Jesus, has declared, the Church is in a process of "readapting the faith, the dogmatic and ecclesiastical values, to a new culture." Paul VI has offered a "greater liberty in the life of the Church and, therefore, in the life of each of its children; that is, there are fewer legal obligations and fewer internal inhibitions." In that same declaration on July 9, 1969 the Pope explained that, "The significance of that Christian liberty which so attracted the first generation of Christians when they were exempt from the Mosaic law and its complicated rites will be encouraged."

In spite of this, Rome watered the quagmire. Its hesitations disheartened and exasperated not only the Young European Church; it disturbed the Young Latin American Church as well. Since the material which the Shadow-Synod studied produced strong consternation in the Roman Curia, future activity of the Congregation for the Propagation of the Faith may be excessive, and the effective excommunication which Cardinal Franjo Seper recommended is likely. If Paul VI can maintain his reasonableness in the midst of the Vatican bureaucracy and its intrigues, to the point of making real those promises of "greater liberty in the life of the Church," the "Revolution of John XXIII" will fully come to life. Then the epoch of John will mark one of the most brilliant eras in the history of the Church, comparable only to the beautiful springtime of its beginnings.

With such Christian liberty never again would there be a repitition of the inquisitorial repressions experienced in Cuernavaca or directed against Father Salvador Freixedo of Puerto Rico, to cite only two of the most clamorous cases of brutality. The Dutch Catechism could be analyzed, disseminated, and judged without fear and with such clear intelligence as that displayed by a Colombian, Eduardo Cárdenas, in the *Revista Javeriana* of Bogotá in August, 1969. The young clergy wants to engage in dialogue with the hierarchy and with those who make up the broad base of the Church without the restraints that impede active and healthful participation in the decisions related to any human endeavor. They have opposed the depersonalization that characterizes hermetic, vertical systems. Rejection of that totalitarian discipline, as well as their reaction to the inadequate understanding of the social *aggiornamento*, engendered their rebellion.

The Seven Salvadorean bishops, with the Archbishop of San Salvador, Luis Chávez y González in the lead, are prime examples of that type of incomprehension. No one denies that El Salvador's greatest problem, in addition to the concentration of landownership, is the population explosion. El Salvador has the greatest percentage growth of population in the world, and the greatest concentration of landownership, proportionately in Latin America. The obvious result is the emigration of poor peasants in large numbers. The Salvadorean hierarchy has declared that it is prepared "to receive from the landowners lands which they might voluntarily want to cede for transfer in a technical, orderly, and just manner to the peasants." That was how the Salvadorean hierarchy interpreted the encyclical *Populorum Progressio*.

In considering objectively the actual Latin American situation, it becomes evident that in intellectual matters, scientific research, and the pastoral mission, the post-conciliar priesthood can find the best ways to achieve the *aggiornamento* in the orientations and style which Bishop Sergio Méndez Arceo has stressed in his Cuernavaca diocese, and in Father Ernesto Cardenal's experiment in the Great Lake of Nicaragua as well.

Progressive priests differ about tactics for the rapid and effective social *aggiornamento* in the Latin American Church. Cardinal Landázuri Ricketts of Peru clearly perceived and admitted that he was in favor of determining a way to meet the urgency for social change in Latin America which, according to him, must be achieved by Catholics of this generation. In his opinion, "the alternative for responsible men of our generation is not between the maintenance of the present situation and change; such a position is obsolete. We all agree on the necessity for rapid and profound change. The choice now is in the means for carrying out the urgent task. An abnormal situation prevails in Latin America where the dignity of the human being is ignored and where large masses await the signal for redemption."

The passive resistance which the Bishop of Olinda and Recife wanted to organize seems to be the tactical solution. It would be tragic—even disastrous—to confront the professional violence of the establishment with the lesser fire-power of the exploited. The case of Vietnam is invoked in contradicting Helder Cámara. The argument is fallacious. If we condemn the war in Vietnam, it is reasonable to ask why we should favor military intervention in our continent while other means of struggle are available. The logistics of the situation—the fact that China borders Vietnam and the Soviet Union is on the same continent—are disregarded. Also, those who base their delirium, or their desperation, on those remote possible sources of help forget Latin America's geographical position. Father Camilo Torres must be taken as a symbol of the struggle of the progressive clergy in Latin America, not as an example. United States military power rules out armed rebellion. That assumption, confirmed recently from Guatemala to Argentina, has led the progressive clergy to become acutely anti-Yankee. The most active members judge the Latin American case from the only angle which our perspective permits. This was the source of the rebuffs which Rockefeller, personal envoy of President Nixon, experienced on his three trips to Latin America during the first half of 1969.

At times Rome gives the impression that it is abandoning the vanguard of the Latin American Church. By spreading discord among its better ranks, it loses ground. At other times it gives the impression of stimulating the innovators to glorious, conciliar interpretations. Waves of pure air enter the churches, and the occupants of the velvet pews are swept toward the door, frowning and threatening.

Rome's backing and filling led Paul VI to speak of crisis within the Church. In Latin America there definitely exist two well-defined positions, difficult to harmonize—that of the Old Church, institutional, triumphant, and that of the Young Church, rebellious against oppression and authoritarianism. The former sleeps in its ecclesiastical benefices, complicit in social injustice, with a conformist tradition of almost five centuries of legal force and victory. The latter places its youthful rebellion on the side of social justice, just as Fray Antonio de Montesinos did in Española for the first time in America one day at the beginning of the sixteenth century.

Ego vox clamantis in deserto, the Young Church calls its first Latin American document. Fray Bartolomé de las Casas related how the powerful, on hearing Father Antonio de Montesinos speak, "left the church enraged and went to eat, not a very savory meal, but I think a very bitter one. They did not pay further attention to the friars, for they understood now that to discuss this with them would serve no purpose. They agreed, as a matter of fact, to write to the King by the first ship about how those friars who had come to the island had shocked the world by spreading new doctrine."

Epilogue

The *aggiornamento* of John XXIII brought at first a beneficial burst of hopes, enthusiasms, and much bitter suffering, but, from the very beginning of its introduction into the sclerotic arteries of the Latin American Church, it gradually subsided into apathy. An overall view shows that the renovating impulse with its strong and at times discouraging pressures on the hardened walls of the ecclesiastical establishment had to rely on unusual means to attain its goals. The rigidity of canonical structures, produced by four centuries of obsessive preoccupation with and distortion of symbols, left no room for nor permitted the vigorous circulation of that impulse.

Thus progressive Catholic sectors found that they were forced to seek other channels for expressing themselves openly and freely, at least as a premise for their ingenuousness or their disenchantment. The marginal courses taken by the renovators in their zeal for transforming the Latin American Church appear at present as an extensive repertory of political tactics or evasions related to nationalism with the official option for change available to each one of the governments in that southern part of the Western Hemisphere. On their part the traditionalist currents of the Church have maintained their ancient positions. If in some cases and on some occasions they have varied them, the object has been to strengthen their convictions and their bonds with the most recalcitrant feudal expressions of the oppressing groups.

From that point of view, attempts at analyzing on a continental scope the transformation of the Catholic mentality for which

Vatican Council II tried to provide a favorable atmosphere, seems fraught with risks; that is, applying fixed schemes to the whole is open to question. Latin America offers a varied mosaic of realities based on the degree of economic and political development of the individual countries. Nor can a conscientious analysis which aspires to the discovery of irrefutable evidence ignore the marvelous ingredients which reveal features of the diverse levels of the total Latin American ambiguity. At the core of the generalizations which point to Latin America as a homogeneous entity writhe innumerable differences, generally irreconcilable, which lead to glossing over the neglected surface uniformity of our continent, or relegate it to the rhetoric of the OAS and the facility of the good discreditors of sociology. The pious, arbitrary methods of branding the continent with an idyllic human and physical landscape have been applied—the persistence of the "noble savage" mythology—making it impossible for the popularized gnostological standards to be accommodated to their various environmental and psychical realities. Commitment to such fixations customarily leads to costly errors which are equally exemplified by too many inter-American creations of the United States—the Alliance for Progress, not to look very far—and of Castro, the apostolic liberator, clothed by the Cuban regime in its early idealism in the war-like initials of OLAS, Organization for Latin American Solidarity.

The countries in that southern part of the planet are as different from each other as those trying to become united in what is called the Arab World. Their concurrences and growing affinity of interests are not being nourished in the community of language or religion, in their geographic proximity, or in vague historic episodes. Their reciprocal attractions are no longer matters of illusion when consideration is given to their social and economic problems which become frightening patterns of subhuman life for sectors of the population increasing at an impressive rate, each day more deeply immersed in irrationality.

It must be accepted that the Latin American manner of propagating the species has changed little since the Spanish conquest. Ezequiel Martínez Estrada recalls that,

The Indian woman served the white invader for his nocturnal pleasure after an idle day; she gave her blood to the source of weariness and disillusionment, and anguish was born from pleasure. Love was not required, nor fidelity, for male and female were joined physically; when he arose, she went about her long hours of daily chores. Later, many legitimated those unions, rather as an act of contrition or piety than of love. Even until recently committees of priests customarily provided for uniting in heaven those who had been disunited in body and soul."

As love was improvised, so was everything else. What irresponsibility promotes oppresses us: the declining population of the countryside, the concentration of the resentful masses—food for fascism—in the great cities, the immoderate population growth. Apparently Latin American countries are not alone in these critical matters; they can identify with those countries now struggling to consolidate their difficulties in search for remedies through a motley conglomeration of contradictions under the nominal fiction of a Third World.

The revolution in the Church has had a different manifestation in each of the Latin American countries. The Mexican development differed from the Argentinian. It could not be otherwise, for Mexico is the only country in Latin America which in the nineteenth century achieved a liberal revolution which it has maintained, producing from the process a lay state, rare in the Hispanic cultural galaxy. Thus Mexico broke with the medieval Spanish heritage of the colonial era.

The contrary occurred in Argentina. When in March, 1973 the Holy See officially received Dr. Héctor J. Cámpora, then the presidential candidate supported by General Juan Domingo Perón who had been rejected by the Vatican at the time of the military revolt of 1955, it was recognized that the major obstacle in the way of the Argentinian party determined to win by any means at the ballot box had been removed. What may be the similarities between Mexico and Argentina? Mexico is as remote to any *porteño* of good will as many Argentinian political, literary, sporting, or musical modes are to Mexicans to whom they are little less than undecipherable. It is not common for a Buenos Aires citizen to form a theory about Mexico such as that suggested by Julio Cortázar after observing for many hours an axolotl [a larval salamander found in Mexico] in the humid aquarium of the Jardin des Plantes in Paris: "Behind those Aztec features, inexpressive but nevertheless implacably cruel, what image awaited its hour?" Cortázar maintained the idea in *La noche boca arriba*. Jorge Luis Borges had already ventured to theorize about Mexico in *La escritura del dios*. But that is another matter. The certainty is, as already indicated—an observation principally valid for the layman's economy—that if the Mexican has survived on dry and arid land, the Argentinian is the grateful victim of his fertile soil.

While living in Mexico the excellent Argentinian poet, Martínez Estrada, determined to untangle the differences and similarities among the Latin American countries. Just as he had finished his work he died suddenly. From among his various inquiries we have selected two. The first concerns land and water relationships between Latin America and Africa "of a kind which transcends the mere conception by which their kinship and destiny are more tightly tied than with Europe." Estrada concluded that "That is the fate of the Caribbean, and today it is not necessary to point it out, for it is obvious." The other high point is his conjecture about the existence of an integrated area of Venezuela, Brazil, Colombia, and Argentina which led him to conclude that "Each one develops its own plan of existence; and their common and universal forces, such as the ecumenical, do not have sufficient power to unify that which the 'division of labor' continually diversifies."

A preamble thus sifted from ideas obviously very much against the grain of what we would call the theme of this book leads us to set forth four areas of domestic affinity in the development of the *aggiornamento* of the Catholic Church in Latin America. Any geographical concept escapes classification through the desire for exactitude, inclining us to an elemental fallacy, and has little to do with accepted formulas for the purpose of Latin American research; thus these formulas enjoy, as this one does, the advantages of an evident modesty.

The areas of ecclesiastical action then decided on are based on actual events, favorable to a classification less capricious (less subjective, I was about to say) than those customarily used for analogous purposes. The revolution of the Church in Latin America in 1973 admits, in accordance with the previous exposition, these four areas: the compromise assumed with the social transformations directed by civil power upheld by the will of the majority; armed resistance against the violence of the classic institutions; indifference cultivated with skillful nicety or through relatively dishonorable devices used by those who unlawfully exercise economic and political power which inhibits the uninformed. And in the fourth place, there is the Mexican way.

The first has been represented by the cleverest and most clearheaded forces of the Churches of Chile and Peru; the second by the small unorganized, radical groups in Uruguay, Colombia, and Argentina who have fallen to the temptation of ephemeral glory which the holocaust of unequal combat provides; the third is recognized best in the Brazilian euphoria of foreign investments and by the Panamanian regime's utilizing as a popular entertainment the cruel colonial enclave of the United States in its country, which serves the regime as a midwife to nationality. The Mexican case is unique. Let us follow the outlined order.

Revolution by the Democratic Route

Early in 1970 Cardinal Juan Landázuri Ricketts, Archbishop of Lima, abandoned his palace on the most elegant avenue in the ancient viceregal capital. Many years before his residence had been the gift of a prominent Peruvian family. Landázuri was installed with necessary household goods in a modest house located in a plebian neighborhood. That gesture of austerity would have lacked significance had it not been noted that four canons renounced subventions which, by an agreement dating from independence, dignitaries of the Peruvian Church had received from the State. The canons excused their action by saying that they did not wish to enjoy economic privilege in the midst of poverty and, at the same time, be subjected to a dependency on the State prejudicial to their pastoral mission. Weeks before, priests in ONIS *(Oficina*

Nacional de Información Social) had joined with their colleagues
to take over churches for workers on strike. They stated that a
solution for labor problems could be obtained only with the complete transformation of political, economic, and social structures
of their country. The new military government began to have
problems.

When the General Law of Industry was promulgated on July
27, 1971, nationalizing all foreign capital enterprises in Peru and
providing for progressive worker participation in them up to fifty
per cent of the company capital, it seemed to the progressive clergy
no more than a token gesture. They asked that all means of production become social property. Juan Velasco's military government was considered reactionary. The Church officially announced
that it would initiate an educational effort among adults "to put
them in tune with the structural transformations which Peru
requires."

The tension grew to such a degree that the Auxiliary Bishop of
Lima, Monsignor Luis Bambarén, was detained with other
priests—one from the United States—accused of acting against
the public order. The upper level of the hierarchy raised its voice:
"Everyone knows about the social restlessness and the work of
Monsignor Bambarén who has always collaborated with every sort
of promotion for the needy classes initiated by the Church as well
as the State. In the face of this arbitrary act the Church of Lima,
acting in conjunction with the just demands of the people, raises
its most energetic protest and demands immediate solution of this
case, since it affects the parish of the City of God and the members
of the Parochial Council."

The government sensed the risk. President Velasco Alvarado
responded immediately that "Our country is Catholic. Our people
are Catholic, and the members of the government are Catholic.
The clergy are helping us; they support the revolutionary process.
The clergy and the government are united. No problem exists; we
are firmly united."

It is possible to designate May 13, 1973, when the Chief of
State made that declaration, as the day when the Peruvian revolution began to accelerate. Peasants, workers, intellectuals demanded

it. The progressive clergy stood at the front, seconded by the hierarchy with Cardinal Landázuri at their head. Monsignor Carlos Santiago Burke, Bishop of Chimbote, a fishing port, explained the situation: "We want the Church to be identified with the people's struggle against exploitation, hunger, poverty, humiliation, inhuman treatment, and injustice." That prelate, a native of the United States, added, "In the past we have put much effort into works of benevolence which, in spite of our good intentions, limited the poor to being passive receivers. In spite of our desire to help, we have contributed to making beggars of people who ought to be dignified and proud."

The United States Department of State became uneasy with good reason. It placed the Rand Corporation in charge of an investigation. The experts reported that the Peruvian Catholic Church was becoming more and more engaged in the revolutionary process through pressure of radical members of religious orders on the military government. In effect, their involvement was increasing. The Vatican itself had to step back in the case of the Bishop of Puno, Monsignor Julio González Ruiz, accused by his enemies of sexual obsession, heresy, and anti-papalism. The Peruvian Church, however, defended him. The Holy See filed the case and restored his see to the Bishop of Puno. Pope Paul VI received him in private audience.

The Rand Corporation did not exaggerate in its statement about the radicalism of the Peruvian religious. The Order of St. Dominic was added in January, 1973 to others in the Church supporting the revolution. Dominican provincials indicated that it was necessary to follow closely the political and economic aspects of the public effort because "It is not possible to speak of salvation in the name of the Church without becoming involved in these matters."

With such popular bases and stimuli, the Peruvian regime has been able to follow discreetly, without trepidation, the work of transforming the foundations of a society which had always been characterized by irritants producing an unbalanced state of affairs. From that point of view Peru has been supporting its major causes in international organizations.

Farther south, in the midst of a presidential campaign, the

Chilean bishops issued a letter opposing the "capitalist structure which goes against the dignity of the individual," and reiterated their sympathy for agrarian reform because the Church "considers that the people of the countryside suffer anguish and oppression, and does not consider Christian the difference between master and laborer." What remains for the orators of the left to say? Traditionalists attacked Cardinal Raúl Silva Henríquez by repeating Marxist labels which cannot withstand the least analysis.

On the triumph of Salvador Allende, the Chilean bishops recognized that the supporters of the President-elect "evince great expectations and show a constructive spirit." They observed, "The Chilean people want to continue the regime and the type of freedom for which they have been struggling for one hundred sixty years. They want to keep and defend what they have fought for— the right to think, to make their ideas known to others, to organize themselves, but at the same time, they want that freedom broadened and perfected."

El Siglo, organ of the Chilean Communist party, received with cordiality the episcopal communication and emphasized in an editorial the paragraph which stated that "We have cooperated and wish to cooperate in the changes, especially those which favor the poorest. We know that the changes are difficult and entail great risks for everyone. We understand what it costs to give up some privileges. Therefore it is fitting to call attention to the teachings of Christ regarding the need for brotherhood among men which requires impartiality and better distribution of material wealth."

Paul VI sent his benedictions in a message to Allende and expressed his desires for the government's success which Cardinal Silva Henríquez delivered when he visited the socialist leader. The president-elect thanked him publicly, reiterating that he was not a believer. A month before taking possession of the presidency, he made clear his position with respect to the Church: "The points of view of believers and unbelievers will be fully respected in Chile. When a man has no work and is hungry, it does not matter what his religion may be."

On the day of his succession President Allende attended a *Te Deum* at which the Cardinal of the Metropolitan Cathedral officiated. Monsignor Silva Henríquez read before the new Chief of State a sermon containing the following significant paragraph:

Having recently received the standard of the supreme mandate of the nation, the President has chosen to come to this temple and participate in this service of thanks. It is a gesture—an ennobling one—of delicate respect for the religious values of the Chilean people, represented here in the pastors and ministers of their several communities of faith.

The Cardinal said to the Cuban journalists who had come to Santiago to attend Allende's assumption of office and whom he received in special audience that the Chilean Church supported the basic reforms contained in the program of the *Unidad Popular*, political organization of the Marxist parties which had won in the presidential election with Allende. Concerning the Church's relations with socialist states, the Cardinal told them that socialism has enormous Christian values which in many ways make it superior to capitalism. And he added for the press of Havana, "We must effectively collaborate with men of good will who are trying to better the world and must not link ourselves with transitory economic and social organizations and institutions, many of them already outmoded."

The Salesians, members of the order to which the Cardinal belongs, organized journeys to offer a minimal but sufficient overall presentation of Marxism. With such studies the Salesians sought to discover the implications of Marxism in the Chilean situation and to outline some lines of political and pastoral strategy with regard to the situation strongly influenced by that doctrine, especially among the young.

It was estimated in 1971 that three-fourths of the Chilean clergy felt more attached to the extreme left than to the conservative sectors. In a special study on that point, Georgetown University, a Jesuit institution, explained that more than half of Catholic Chileans accept a friendly collaboration with Marxists, and a considerable part reject the Marxist doctrine but accept the dialogue with the disciples of the author of *Das Kapital*. In any case, sixty priests in Santiago signed a document in which they asked the Church to put an end "to the official condemnation of Marxism, leaving without force the premise Pius XII had set forth to the effect that Marxism was essentially perverse." Also in that document they requested that Marxism "no longer consider Christianity the opiate of the people and cease presenting it as a capitalist conditioning influence."

Monsignor Sergio Contreras Navia, spokesman for the Chilean hierarchy at the Universal Synod of Bishops called together by the Vatican in October 1971 stated that "Chile is a country that follows the democratic route to socialism." Without a break in his voice, he continued to say to the two hundred eleven members of the Synod convened by Paul VI, "Marxism and its consequences ought to be considered in the light of the faith and the signs of the times. The fact cannot be ignored that today many Christians are inclined toward Marx's theories; therefore, it is necessary to study the problems so that we may give them an adequate Christian response."

Two months after the Roman synod, Fidel Castro arrived in Chile. Priests surrounded him; he chatted with the Cardinal. At the end of his interview with Silva Henríquez, the Cuban Prime Minister commented, "Certainly there are differences between Marxists and Christians, but there are agreements as well. Christians and Marxists can and ought to work together for the liberation of the people." He explained in his own style that "The rapprochement between revolutionaries and Christians is a very important strategy because there are a great many Christians among the Latin American masses who are dedicated to the revolutionary effort . . . and we attach importance to that fact."

At the beginning of 1972 numerous Chilean priests offered to go to Cuba to participate as volunteers in the sugar cane harvest. Castro pointed out that between the doctrines they propounded and Marxism "there are no contradictory objectives." He recalled that "If there have been artificial barriers for political reasons, these are gradually disappearing, thanks, among other things, to the action of progressive Latin American priests." With regard to Cuba, he cleared the rubbish out of the way by saying, "Latin American priests can help the Cuban Revolution by elaborating a definite policy of rapprochement with the Church in Cuba itself."

As the Chilean socialist government accelerated the process of economic and social transformation, foreseeable conflicts and problems arose: food scarcities caused by reconversions of property and of agricultural production, and the increase in urban demand resulting from the greater buying power of the popular classes; contraction of external credit; flight of capital; international blockade on the sale of nationalized copper; calculated decline in the rate of manufacturing; management lockout from which the country suffered a loss of about 100 million dollars; strikes by non-union transportation workers; opposition in the universities. Demands on the people required too many sacrifices of freedom. In that context of difficulties, with the opposition taking full advantage of them, the Congressional election occurred.

In those elections on March 4, 1973 Allende's government increased its position by more than seven per cent while the opposition Electoral Alliance lost almost eleven per cent. What should be done? The right in Chile launched an effort to conquer the armed forces and the clergy for a *coup d'etat.* The opposition had strong and ample forces at its disposal, both national and foreign, and it does not skimp. Something seemed to have promoted its purpose. Would it succeed? The ecclesiastical hierarchy suggested that the country was on the verge of civil war.

The Broken Guerrillas

The armed resistance groups in Peru have indicated their attitude by supporting the programs of the government headed by President Velasco Alvarado. After retreating from the country to the city, decimated, Brazilian guerrillas succumbed one after the other in Rio de Janeiro, São Paulo, Fortaleza, Recife, and Aracajú. In September 1971 Carlos Lamarca, discouraged, yielded in the fields of Bahía. Mass detentions have become the order of the day. Torture in the jails has taken care of the rest. Censorship guarantees the tranquility of good consciences.

In Uruguay the *Frente Amplio,* a leftist group, lost the most recent election. Under the state of emergency giving war-time powers to Pacheco Arceo, president at that time, the extermination of the Tupumaros began. Scores who escaped death have been cast into the penitentiaries.

Uruguayan Catholics are divided with respect to the urban guerrillas. Traditionalists accuse the Archbishop Coadjutor of Montevideo, Monsignor Parteli, of supporting subversion. When they are more compassionate, they are of the opinion that he "is a fool useful to the Communists." The police found the Jesuit Justo Asiáin and the Methodist minister Emilio Castro together and detained them for being linked to the Tupumaros. The Apostolic Nuncio, Monsignor Sepinski, condemned the kidnapping of the United States official, Dan Mitrione, on detached service in Uruguay, because "the Church condemns violence." A group of Christian communities got out of the difficulty by saying, "Their position inclines toward the diplomatic world, but their mission is above all evangelical. Therefore, their voice must be raised primarily for the defense of our many brothers who suffer from a different form of violence—the sort that promotes hunger and unemployment—which undermines all just liberties, perpetuates conditions of subhuman life, limits the 'progress of the people' subjected to imperialism and to its unconditional servitors. The violence which shocks us today is only a consequence of this primary and fundamental violence. No one can deny it."

The Tupumaros are still victims in encounters with the army and the police. Others succumb from maltreatment in prison. On one occasion guerrillas took refuge in the Church of Our Lady of Lourdes. The government closed two newspapers, and students protested by taking over the Montevideo Cathedral. Lucía Topolansky was captured. Raúl Séndic, founder and leading theorist of the Tupumaros, was arrested in the capital after two hours of random shooting; he was taken to the penal institution of Punta Carretas gravely wounded in the mouth by a projectile. The United States missionary, Eugene L. Stockwell, sent a letter to the *New York Times* stating that the news of the capture of Raúl Séndic, Tupumaro leader, might make some people believe in the return of law and order to Uruguay. He noted that the Tupumaro rebellion might be breaking up, but the main thing in that country was the governmental repression violating human rights in a most brutal way. The missionary condemned the continuation by the United States of economic and military aid to Uruguay which in his view compromised the United States. The new president, Juan M. Bordaberry, rose victorious from that little known and degrading tragedy. The military made clear what it expected for its cooperation.

On the other side of the Río Plata the guerrillas disappeared for other reasons. When the more veteran Peronist forces joined the urban terrorists of the left, the rank-and-file Argentinian priests launched themselves wholeheartedly into the struggle against the militarist government. They were censured as communists. The Bishop of Rioja, Monsignor Angeletti, responded, "We are tired of the commonplace charge that any attempt to free our country from the established order indicates support of Marxist ideology." The arrest of Monsignor Francisco Vicentín, Archbishop of Corrientes, was ordered. The priests of the "Third World" organization sanctioned violence publicly. The episcopate reproached them on the grounds that, "Accepting violence as a means for liberating the poor in the shortest possible time is not fitting nor legitimate for any group of priests, either in their priestly character or through the social doctrine of the Church which opposes violence, or through the means of social revolution which it implies."

Detention of Fernando Carbone and Fulgencio Alberto Rojas, two priests belonging to the "Third World," accused respectively of participation in the kidnapping and assassination of ex-President Pedro Eugenio Aramburu and an assault on a town, precipitated a division in the Argentinian Church. At the religious burial of the principals responsible for Aramburu's death, the priest who spoke for the "Third World" exalted the two terrorists, who had been riddled with bullets by the police, and held them up as examples.

The generals felt obliged to make a change in the management of the militarist government. Overwhelming popular protest forced General Alejandro Lanusse to call for elections. The Peronist candidate, Dr. Héctor J. Cámpora, won by a large majority. Animosities subsided. What will Cámpora do in the *Casa*

Rosada? What will he be thinking when he is in Olivos [the private home of the president]? The answers will reveal whether this is anything more than the lull of a truce.

Colombia is another country with guerrillas. Even before Camilo Torres appeared on the scene, some Colombian clerics had taken on a radical attitude within the most traditionalist Church in the Catholic world, not forgetting Spanish addiction to the *Generalísimo*. Furthermore, the extreme position of the Colombian Church is not the invention of the hierarchy. Its attachment to the postulates in force before Vatican Council II is shared by the devoted masses of peasants, workers, and the middle class. The military strongly favor it. It is upheld, in other words, by an overwhelming popular concensus. All the political parties support it, even those following the leftist line. No one argues the Church's right to participate in active politics, and no one understands its humility when it refuses to arbitrate the differences between the chiefs of a local political group, its brother parishioners.

Hence it was unusual when a bishop, Monsignor Gerardo Valencia Cano, dared to confess in public that, "Definitely, I proclaim myself, with the companions of Golconda, revolutionary and socialist because we cannot remain indifferent to the capitalist structure which is producing among the Colombian people the most tremendous frustrations and injustices." That Bishop of Buenaventura, a port on the Pacific coast, was actively seconded by the Bishop of Facatativá in the Andean altiplano, Monsignor Raúl Zambrano Camader. Those two prelates inspired the Golconda group of young and progressive priests. Many of them became tired of meditating about a theology of liberation, and some, fretfully, hung up their soutanes while others guided by the spirit of Camilo Torres joined the guerrillas.

There is no doubt, however, that the Lord is a traditionalist in Colombia. On January 20, 1972 the airplane carrying Monsignor Valencia Cano crashed to the earth. Eleven months later the two-motored plane carrying Monsignor Zambrano Camader, the other progressive prelate, suffered the same fate. Without leaders, the Golconda group began to disappear without notice and without

173

glory. On its part, the government relied on the vortex of the jungle to devour slowly, one by one, the guerrilla priests. For in Colombia the jungle is also traditionalist.

The Indifferent Ones

If we begin with the datum that the Latin American continent is inhabited by 250 million people, 90 per cent of whom profess the Catholic religion, we may venture the opinion that the renovation of the Church agreed upon by Vatican Council II has been regarded with indifference by the bureaucrats garbed in long Roman robes and safely preserved in the Vatican. Those revisions and instructions have managed to infiltrate even very high ecclesiastical levels in Latin America where they have been interpreted according to the temperament and worldly interests of each. The rank-and-file clergy understood the conciliar schemas as a call to arms, as a gratifying recognition in the front line trenches that not even the Holy See is exempt from the sinister incursions of the devil. With regard to this point, Latin American seminarians have shown that they are not exceptions within the clinical framework of the education imparted in the region.

Brazil, the most extensive country with the largest population in this little known part of the world, demonstrates the situation. The vacuum or the wrath generated in his surroundings by the words of Monsignor Helder Cámara, Bishop of Olinda and Recife, provides confirmation. More clearly than anyone else in Latin America, he has understood the transcendency of the renewal of Christian mental attitudes and conduct. All in vain.

Brazil has been enveloped by a vicariously articulated period of progress and the enjoyment of its very rapid development. Helder Cámara's voice has been muffled by the noise with which unprecedented projects and accomplishments have been presented to the public. Brazilians provide satisfying figures for the OAS economists such as those showing the increase in the gross national product, a spiraling per capita income, an increase in exports, a great influx of foreign investments, growth in internal savings, and a vertiginous increase in industrial production. For whom? For what? Two people know the answers: President Richard M. Nixon, who declared the Brazilian regime an example for Latin America, designating it the natural leader of our countries, and Bishop Helder Cámara who has observed the increasing misery of millions of his compatriots in the quadrilateral of hunger.

With more than eight million square kilometers and with fabulous natural resources, Brazil by its own specific weight will determine the destinies of South America in the coming years. It shares boundaries with all the South American countries except Chile. Brazil has received its assignment from the Washington politicos. They are not stupid. By the year 2000 South America will be whatever Brazil may be. What can the weak, musical voice of Helder Cámara accomplish in the face of such definite and well planned designs?

There are numerous ways to deflect the attention of the people. One, long recognized is the agitation of nationalistic sentiments, with the knowledge that in the end all will remain the same.

Panamanians rebelled in common indignation on learning that the Colombian priest, Héctor Gallego, founder and promoter of a cooperative for poor peasants in the Province of Veraguas, had been kidnapped. The archbishop of Panama, Monsignor Marcos McGrath, had given them the news and had informed them of what had occurred. "Father Gallego and other priests of the region had been subject to attacks, each more serious than the one before." That post-conciliar priest had organized the plain people of Veraguas; he had awakened their consciousness concerning the injustice of their arrangements with middlemen and the great landowners; he had patiently taught them their rights and pointed out their oppressors. Throughout his extensive parish, he preached for an equitable distribution of land. It was asserted that he had died of tortures inflicted by the authorities. In order to allay the allegations, the government exonerated those accused by some who had witnessed the outrage of having perpetrated it. Officials and sub-officials of the National Guard remain at large.

Where was Father Gallego? The lack of a reply raised heavy black clouds of doubt. A storm was imminent. Archbishop Mc-

Grath in a pastoral letter called for a parade of protest with a governmental investigation; the Bishop of Veraguas, Monsignor Martín Legarra, stated in another pastoral letter that "The proper desire to know the truth about the kidnapping or disappearance of Father Gallego has not been satisfied by the declarations of the Attorney General of the nation." Monsignor McGrath officiated at solemn masses before great crowds to extol "Gallego's virtues as man and priest and to redeem his name from the defamations which have been made to discredit his meritorious work." Confrontation between the Church and the military government almost reached the breaking point. The Vatican intervened. The colonels understood: they opened the floodgates of national feeling.

Inequity in the treatment of Panama by the United States has continued effectively to build up an arsenal of suppressed emotions. The canal cost the United States 300 million dollars. Ships which have passed through it since 1923 have paid one billion 14 million dollars. For its concession in perpetuity the United States assumed the obligation in 1904 of paying annually "to the head of the government in power" $250,000; in 1936 that payment was increased to $430,000. [Panama currently receives $2,300,000 a year.] In 1955 the United States began to pay Panama one million dollars annually. The profits from the canal have recently been about 700 million dollars a year. More important, the Zone provides the United States with locations for 14 military bases, keys to the Pentagon's hemispheric strategy.

The Army School of the Americas of the United States and the general barracks of the Eighth Group of Special Forces, better known as the "Green Berets," are located at Fort Gulick in Cristóbal Bay on the Atlantic side. According to the periodical, *Army Digest*, at those installations various methods for defeating an insurgent in the field of battle as well as the functions of the civil-military action in an insurrection are taught. According to *Nacla*, a Pentagon publication, that school has instructed more than 26,000 Latin American officers and soldiers in various military specialties. Ernesto Guevara, Camilo Torres, Carlos Lamarca, Raúl Séndic could all have testified to the efficiency of that instruction. The technicians trained at Fort Gulick can boast of having exterminated the principal guerrilla centers in Latin America; without doubt there is no way out for their remnants. With good reason, Panamanians hope the canal will be turned over to them some day with the benefits rightfully theirs. General Omar Torrijos, their strong man, expressed that view when he said, "It is certain that we ought to be at the service of the world, but it is not fair that we pay for it at the cost of supporting a colonial enclave containing a strategic command." General Torrijos was able to voice a complaint, having succeeded in getting the Security Council of the United Nations to meet in Panama in March 1973 to deal with the matter. All the Latin American chancelleries except those of Brazil and Nicaragua united in support of the Panamanian complaint before that tribunal. Only the United States veto of the final resolution of the Security Council prevented the resolution of the conflict in accordance with the exigencies of General Torrijos. The scenery having been dismantled, the Panamanian Chancellor declared that the matter rested there.

The corpse of Father Gallego has not appeared. Along their pathways people sing *coplas* composed in his memory. Gallego has become another legend.

Mexico

The catalyst of the reform movements within the Mexican Church has been Bishop Méndez Arceo, Bishop of Cuernavaca, the beautiful capital of Morelos. While he was devoting himself to canonical and liturgical issues, he aroused scarcely any domestic attacks from those informed about them. In those areas his conflicts were with the Vatican Curia, and the tribulations they caused him were well known. He stimulated the intelligent sociological expressions of Father Ivan Illich and protected the Benedictine Lemercier, caught in the fires of psychoanalysis, from the witch hunt directed at him. From those activities rooted in theology Monsignor Méndez Arceo began to turn his attention to political participation. The consequences of his entry into the secular world were immediately forthcoming. Two wings formed within the Mexican Church: the progressives who backed him, and the traditionalist who followed Monsignor Octaviano Márquez y Toriz, Archbishop of Puebla. Their reciprocal attacks were as virulent as those in any other Latin American country. Through historical experience that dishonorable and cruel quarrel put Mexican liberalism on guard.

Méndez Arceo, who had declared himself a socialist and had journeyed openly to Cuba, thought that for his post-conciliar ideas, the situation in the State of Morelos made it a splendid arena of political action awaiting his redemptive word: hard-working peasants who were followers of Emilio Zapata, and Cuernavaca workers and those in the sugar mills who seemed to be distant from their union leaders. Mexican students continued to be deluded by the night of Tlatelolca [occasion of student demonstrations in Mexico City with a number killed by government forces] and those of Puebla were rebellious. Monsignor Méndez Arceo entered the determined struggle of those sectors. In his opinion the philosophy of the Mexican Revolution had grown old and, in the process of political biology, was at the stage of throttling any possibility of change or of the realization of its ideals and programs. He estimated that the clamors against the rigidity adopted in recent years by the party in power ought to be led in the cities and byways by the progressive group of clergy who had become inspired in their almost daily declarations to the newspapers.

The students ignored the invitations which the prelate of Cuernavaca issued them on their own university grounds. They were determined to destroy thoroughly the National Autonomous University of Mexico, a task in which they have been laboriously engaged for the last fifty years in order to obtain an institution suited to the revolutionary idea of opening higher education to the popular classes. Then when Monsignor Méndez Arceo began to contend with the CTM [*Confederación de Trabajadores Mexicanos*] for control of the Morelos unions, the workers of Cuernavaca chose a Sunday morning for protesting his purpose. The Bishop collided with Fidel Velásquez, veteran union leader, master in a somewhat uncommon degree of the abilities which made the Mexican politician one with few peers in that most disputatious occupation.

The Bishop of Cuernavaca began to follow a course running counter to Mexico's history, making the Constitution frown. The explanation does not go beyond knowledge acquired at first hand: when the Church became involved in the past century in the French intervention and supported the empire of Maximilian of Hapsburg, as an institution it was a recognized participant in the defeat inflicted by the Mexican people on the foreign invaders. Napoleon III and Pius IX did not believe it possible even after General François Bazaine's defeat.

Nineteenth century Mexican thinkers and fighters of the Reform (the advanced political ideas of the nineteenth century at least merit being known), among whom Benito Juárez stood out in the glory of his own merits, consolidated the liberal principles in the Fundamental Charter of 1857 which established the separation of Church and State. Through the Constituent Congress of Querétaro, the Revolution of 1910 retained the structural doctrines of a lay state, confirmed the liberty of conscience, and reiterated the prohibition, even to Juárez, of the excessive economic and educational monopolies which had supported the medieval, absolute dominion of the high ecclesiastical hierarchies over society and the State in other countries of Latin America. Article 130 of the Constitution now in force, which continues historically Article 123 of the Constitution of 1857, clearly sets forth the fields of action of the institutional Church of Mexico. The not inconsiderable attachment of the progressive clergy to the popular aspirations for betterment become viable and enticing to the degree that its representatives confine themselves to the fields of activity which history indicates and the basic juridical regulations of the nation lay down.

The Mexican government, inaugurated in 1970, which has become known for its dynamic acceptance of the generational shift, has opened the floodgates checking analysis and criticism. It has ventilated the situation by the attitude implicit in its modern approach and treatment of national problems, and it has removed impediments from the encouraging perspectives through recognition of the ideological plurality linking Mexico with the contemporary world. Thus, the differences in the Church between "progressives" and "traditionalists" have been limited to those who wish to take part in an internal debate which, on television and in advertisements in the newspapers, rashly unclothe corporative intimacies to the amazement of believers.

Finally, what importance does Rome concede to Latin America in this post-conciliar era of the history of the Church? The Vatican is concerned with reinforcing its walls so that no one again may open a breach in the Holy Gate. That is understandable. There are too many General Rafael Cadornas [Italian general in command when (1870) Rome was taken from the pope] loose in the world. The Holy See meditates. It is more concerned with the East than with Latin America. That is rational. The East will determine the apothegm of its eternity. It weighs. It measures. And it knows our planet will continue navigating through unlimited space, though in what direction, no one knows.

Index

The Revolution of the Latin American Church

Managua, Nicaragua: 82
Marañon, Brazil: 45
Marcos, Bishop Jorge: 42–43
Mariana, Juan de: 5
Maritain, Jacque: 68
Maritain, Raissa: 68
Márquez y Toriz, Monsignor Octaviano (Archbishop of Puebla, Mexico): 178
Martín, Gonzalo: 77
Martínez Estrada, Ezequiel: 161
Mártir, Pedro, of Anglería: 4
Marty, Cardinal François (Archbishop of Paris, France): 137ff.
Marx, Karl: 128, 169
Marxism (Marxists): 14, 18, 20, 43, 55, 56, 66, 100, 168–69
Maryknoll Order of Ossining, N.Y.: 80
Masons: 60
Mater et Magistra (encyclical): 11, 12, 75
Maurer, Cardinal Clemente: 75
Maximilian of Austria: 89, 179
Mayer, Father Paul: 120
MEB: *see Movimiento Educativa de Base*
Medellín, Colombia: 17, 56, 58; Episcopal Conference in, 115ff., 120–21, 155
Meinville, Julio: 60
Mejía, Vicente: 56
Mejía Vilchez, Enrique: 81, 83
Melville, Father Arthur: 80
Melville, Thomas R.: 109
Mena Porte, Aníbal (Archbishop of Asunción, Paraguay): 73
Méndez Arceo, Sergio (Bishop of Cuernavaca, Mexico): 10, 90, 94ff., 157, 179; and reform in Mexico, 177; journey to Chile, 176
Méndez Montenegro, Julio César: 80
Mendoza Hoyos, Hernán: 27
Menéndez Rodríguez, Mario: 109

Mercier, Cardinal Desiderio J.: 90ff.
Mestri, Monsignor Guido del: 111
Mexico: 81, 98, 162, 163, 177; church in, 32ff., 89–118, 162–63, 170–80; Fundamental Charter of 1857, 179
Mier, Fray Servando Teresa: 9
Mitrione, Dan: 171
Monastery of the Resurrection of Santa María Amacatitlan: 90, 95, 96
Montanaro, Sabeno A.: 73
Montesinos, Father Antonio de: 5ff., 159
Montevideo, Ramón María de: 62
Montevideo, Uruguay: 65
Moscow, USSR: 145, 146
Movimiento Educativa de Base (MED—Basic Education Movement): 42
Mozzoni, Humberto (Papal Nuncio, Argentina): 59ff.
Muñoz Duque, Bishop Aníbal (apostolic administrator of Bogotá): 28, 54
Musanta, Monsignor Giovanni: 124
Mutis, Father José Celestino: 8

Nacla (Pentagon publication): 176
Napoleon III: 179
National Autonomous University of Mexico: 118, 178
National Conference of Bishops of Brazil: 45–46
Neruda, Pablo: 67
Netherlands, The: 29
New Granada: 50
New York Times: 171
Nicaragua: 81ff.
Niteroi, Brazil: 39
Nixon, President Richard M.: 33, 71, 158
Nóbrega, Manuel: 6
Nouvelle Revue Theologique (French periodical): 141

Avellaneda, Argentina, previously of Nueva de Julio, Argentina): 60
Querétaro, Mexico: 117
Quetzaltenango, Guatemala: 81

Rahner, Karl: 130ff.
Ramondetti, Father Miguel: 64
Ranchos of Colombian cities: 17
Rand Corporation: 166
Recife, Brazil: 42, 48, 170
Renovationis Causam (Vatican instructive): 97
Rerum Novarum (encyclical): 14, 21
Resende, Joao (Bishop of Belo Horizonte, Brazil): 20
Reuten, Joost: 132
Revista Javeriana (periodical of Bogotá, Colombia): 156
Rio de Janiero, Brazil: 39, 45, 46, 170
Rio Plata, South America: 65, 172
Roa Bastos, Augusto: 70
Rockefeller, Nelson: 71, 84, 158
Rodríguez, Monsignor Benito: 63
Rojas, Fulgencio Alberto: 172
Roman Catholic Church (faith, religion): 4, 5, 8, 106; *see also* Catholic church, church
Roman Congregation of Religious: 96
Roman Curia: 35, 106, 107, 129ff., 139, 140, 156; *see also* Vatican
Rome: 32, 100, 107, 131ff., 140, 158, 180; *see also* Supreme Pontiff, Vatican
Romey, Joseph: 88
Rosario, Argentina: 17, 63
Rossi, Angelo (Bishop of São Paulo, Brazil): 46, 134
Rubin, Ladislas (Bishop in Poland): 131

Sacerdotus Celibatus (encyclical): 25, 124
Saint Gregory the Great: 37

Salazar Green, Juan: 116, 117
Salto, Colombia: 65
San Felipe Neri (convent): 175
San Obrero, José: 61
San Salvador, Brazil: 39
Sánchez, Manuel (Archbishop of Concepción, Chile): 69
Sandino, Augusto César: 8
Sandoval, Alonso: 6
Santa Fe, Argentina: 59, 62
Santiago, Chile: 17, 67ff., 168; cathedral of, 34, 37
Santiago Burke, Carlos (Bishop of Chimbate, Peru): 166
São Paulo, Brazil: 39, 40, 170
Schema XIII (The Church and the Modern World): 113
Schiellebeek, Edward: 131, 138
Secretariat of Episcopal Conference: 42
Séndic, Raúl: 171, 176
Senegal, Africa: 49
Seper, Cardinal Franjo (President of the Congregation for the Propagation of the Faith): 32, 107, 110, 130, 156
Sepinski, Monsignor (Apostolic Nuncio to Uruguay): 171
Sepúlveda, Juan Ginés de: 4
Shadow Synod: 32, 133ff., 156; *see also* European Assembly of Priests
Sierra Leone, Africa: 49
Silva Hernández, Cardinal Raúl (Chile): 66, 69, 167ff.
Smarth, William: 88
Society of Jesus: 4ff., 71, 72, 154; *see also* Arrupe, Father Pedro
Socorro, Colombia: 50
Soldini, Argentina: 63
Solentiname, lake in Nicaragua: 81, 83
Somoza, Anastasio: 82
Sonnet, Ernesto: 63
Spain: 4, 49, 50, 148, 150, 151
Spellman, Cardinal Francis (New